CLIMBING:
From Gym to Crag

CLIMBING:
From Gym to Crag

BUILDING SKILLS FOR REAL ROCK

S. Peter Lewis and Dan Cauthorn

SWAN·HILL
PRESS

Copyright © 2000

First published in the UK in 2000
by Swan Hill Press, an imprint of Airlife Publishing Ltd

Previously published in the United States by The Mountaineers Books

British Library Cataloguing-in-Publication Data
A catalogue record for this book
is available from the British Library

ISBN 1 84037 251 6

The information in this book is true and complete to the best of our
knowledge. All recommendations are made without any guarantee on
the part of the Publisher, who also disclaims any liability incurred in
connection with the use of this data or specific details.

Printed in the United States of America

Project Editor: Kathleen Cubley
Editor: Kris Fulsaas
Designer: Ani Rucki
Illustrators: Bodell Communications and Electronic Illustrators Group

Cover photograph: *Looking down at climber reaching for a hold, Needles,
California* © Greg Epperson and Adventure Photo & Film
Frontispiece: The Vertical World climbing gym, Seattle, Washington © Don Mason
Chapter openers: page 14: The Vertical World climbing gym, Seattle, Washington
© Don Mason; page 60: *Braincloud*, Golden, Colorado © S. Peter Lewis; page 86:
The Last Unicorn, Whitehorse Ledge, New Hampshire © S. Peter Lewis; page 136:
A Tyrolean Traverse, Cathedral Ledge, New Hampshire © S. Peter Lewis

Swan Hill Press
an imprint of Airlife Publishing Ltd
101 Longden Road, Shrewsbury, SY3 9EB, England
E-mail: airlife@airlifebooks.com
Website: www.airlifebooks.com

♻ Printed on recycled paper

Contents

Acknowledgments 7

Introduction 9
    Indoor Climbing/Outdoor Climbing:
        What's the Difference? 9
    How to Use This Book 10
    A Short History of Rock Climbing:
        How Did Indoor Climbing Come About? 12
    A Note About Safety 13

CHAPTER 1

Indoor Climbing—The Fundamentals

    Equipment 16
    Knots 29
    Signals 35
    Ratings 36
    Frequently Used Moves 39
    Belaying 46
    Training 49

CHAPTER 2

Sport Climbing Outdoors

    Pretrip Planning 63
    Hazard Assessment and Safety Management 63
    Climbing Etiquette 65

Equipment 66
Belaying Outdoors 67
Top-Roping on Fixed Anchors 70
Leading on Fixed Anchors 83

CHAPTER 3

Traditional (Rock) Climbing

Equipment 89
Belay Anchors 96
Outside Moves 114
Traditional Leading 120
Seconding a Pitch 128
Transitions 132

CHAPTER 4

Retreat and an Introduction to Self-Rescue

Equipment 139
Rappelling 139
Lowering 150
Belay Escapes 159
Going Up to Get Down 168

Glossary 173
Index 183

Acknowledgments

Thank you to Casey Newman, Peter Mayfield, and Steve Weitzler for their enthusiastic support of this project when it was in its early stages; to Alec Behr and Quentin Lauradunn of International Mountain Equipment and Richard King of the Cranmore Sports Center for their logistical help; to Dave Kelly for his technical assistance; to Jim Martin, who contributed some outstanding photographs; and a special thanks to Jeremiah Lewis for posing for many of the other pictures.

—Peter Lewis

I'd like to thank Rich Johnston for sharing with me the idea of an indoor climbing gym long before any such facility existed; I am indebted to him for having the commitment to make that idea into reality. If it weren't for rock gyms, this book wouldn't exist.

I also must thank the hundreds of members, climbers, and students whom I met and learned from during my many years working at Vertical World. Numerous climbers, from experts to novices, unknowingly contributed in some way to the substance of this book. Four in particular stand out: Tom Hargis, Karl Kaiyala, Bob Margulis, and Carmel Schimmel. Each taught me in different ways how to articulate and understand the nuances of teaching and training indoor-bred climbers for the challenges of the real world.

Thanks to photographer Jim Martin for his professional touch and sage advice. And finally, thanks to Margaret Foster of The Mountaineers Books and my coauthor, Peter Lewis. Like a hard climb, writing a book is something that is impossible to do alone. Margaret steadfastly supported this project from the start, and it was Peter who took the sharp end when the going got tough and punched it out to the summit.

—Dan Cauthorn

Introduction

Climbing: From Gym to Crag bridges the gap between indoor and outdoor climbing. Ten years ago this book would not have been necessary because most climbers still learned rock climbing on real rock. Since then, however, more and more climbers have been introduced to the thrill and challenge of rock climbing at indoor gyms. Climbing gyms have many things going for them: They are great for training and getting strong, they are a wonderful place to learn movement skills and socialize with other climbers, they require only a minimal amount of equipment, they are incredibly convenient—and the weather is always perfect.

But learning to climb in a gym does not prepare a climber to rock climb outside. The gym environment is so controlled that much of the risk has been eliminated, as well as the need for a thorough understanding of some very basic rock-climbing techniques. If you can tie a figure eight knot and belay, then you can climb safely in the gym. You do not need to know how to build a top-rope anchor, how to protect a pitch that does not have bolts, or how to rappel safely in an emergency. These and many other basic skills that past generations of climbers learned first, now do not need to be learned at all by the gym climber. The gym environment creates climbers who are fit, strong, and capable of doing very hard routes, but their confidence and movement skills do not translate to safe climbing outdoors. Too often climbers unknowingly leave the benign world of the gym and step outside with a false sense of security that puts them at great risk.

INDOOR CLIMBING / OUTDOOR CLIMBING: What's the Difference?

At first glance, a climber making moves up an artificial wall and someone rock climbing on an outdoor cliff look like they are doing the same things. They are using some of the same equipment, their partners are belaying in a similar fashion, the climbers are pulling and pushing the same way. On the surface it seems absurd to devote an entire book to exploring the differences between indoor and outdoor climbing. But things are not always as they first appear. The differences between climbing indoors and climbing outdoors are vast. The indoor environment is highly controlled, nearly all risk has been eliminated, and climbers can be taught all they need to know about the safety systems in a few minutes. The outdoor environment is virtually uncontrolled, all risks are possible, and a climber can spend a lifetime learning the safety systems and still not know it all.

Climbing is unique among the equipment-oriented adventure sports in that the thrills, challenge, and much of the satisfaction can be created in a warehouse. Other sports such as skydiving and white-water boating simply cannot be taught or accomplished inside. Practitioners of these and other outdoor adventure sports that rely heavily on equipment and safety systems have to learn by doing them in their natural environment—usually under the guidance of an accomplished enthusiast or professional instructor. The skills for climbing outdoors are often learned that way also; however, an alarming number of people are learning to climb indoors and then heading outside to climb on their own without a thorough understanding of the hazards or knowledge of the techniques needed to minimize them.

This book is designed to address the differences between climbing indoors and outdoors, and systematically teach the skills necessary to make the transition as safe as possible. However, reading an instructional book and mastering the skills it teaches do not guarantee safety. Climbing is dangerous and every climber must take responsibility for his or her own safety.

HOW TO USE THIS BOOK

The topics in this book are arranged in a continuum beginning with indoor climbing and progressing through climbing outdoors on permanent anchors to traditional climbing without permanent anchors to multipitch traditional climbing, finishing up with a primer on self-rescue techniques. The topics are covered in a logical order, with each chapter building on the techniques taught in the chapters before it. The reader is encouraged to move through the book in an equally logical fashion and not move from one chapter to the next until he or she feels confident in having absorbed and mastered the information.

KEY TRANSITION EXERCISES

Wherever a technique or system is introduced that is either not used indoors or is used in a different fashion outdoors than indoors, the reader will find a Key Transition Exercise. These exercises are designed to teach these transitional techniques from the comfort and safety of the ground. Each exercise uses basic equipment and simple props (for example, trees for anchors) as they walk the reader through the steps. This is a far safer and better method of learning skills than experimenting far off the ground.

To practice the Key Transition Exercises found throughout this book, you will need to create a simulated, two-point belay anchor. Although an entire set was built to take the photos in this book that illustrate these exercises, your setup does not need to be as elaborate. Most of the components can be purchased at your local hardware store. To duplicate the anchor used in the exercise photos, you will need the following items:

two bolt hangers (³/₈-inch by 3-inch screw-eyes or eye-bolts can be substituted)

two ³/₈-inch bolts with washers and nuts, or lag bolts (to fasten the bolt hangers to the wall—not needed if using screw-eyes or eye-bolts)

two pieces of ⁵/₁₆-inch chain, each 8 to 10 inches long

two quick-links (⁵/₁₆-inch-diameter—oval, steel, nongated links, with a locking sleeve)

one lap link (³/₈-inch-diameter)

Next, find a place to build your anchor. You will need a wall or similar structure where you can place your anchor approximately 8 feet above the ground with a simulated ledge to stand on 6 feet below the bolts. The wall of a garage, shed, or barn is ideal, and a picnic table bench or the like can be used to create the ledge. Set the bolt hangers approximately 6 feet above the ledge and 1 foot apart (be certain that the bolts and the structure can support several hundred pounds). Attach one end of each length

A close-up of the two-point anchor created in the studio.

Part of the studio set built to shoot some of the photos in this book.

of chain to a bolt with a quick-link and then connect the bottom links together with the lap link to form the master point.

The reader who begins reading where his or her expertise leaves off, and completes each Key Transition Exercise along the way before trying a new technique outside, will arrive at the end of the book with an understanding of basic outdoor rock-climbing techniques as well as having accomplished some real hands-on practice.

A SHORT HISTORY OF ROCK CLIMBING:
How Did Indoor Climbing Come About?

The history of rock climbing is as old as mountaineering itself. Climbing in the mountains has always involved climbing over rocks and up cliffs. In the early part of the twentieth century, rock climbing began to be practiced as a sport in its own right. Early climbers in Germany and Great Britain in particular pursued rock climbing with a passion—in part because of the lack of high, alpine peaks in those countries—and climbed at remarkably high standards. By the 1920s, rock climbing as a subsport of mountaineering was gaining a foothold in the United States. Many viewed rock climbing as a trivial pursuit when compared to the grandeur and obvious success of standing on a high mountain summit, and it was not until the 1950s that rock climbing began to mature and gain wide acceptance as a sport in its own right. That acceptance helped bring about a surge of interest, and development of specific techniques and equipment helped raise standards dramatically. The United States led the way throughout the '60s

and '70s, to a great extent because of a group of dedicated climbers who made their home in the rock-climbing wonderland of Yosemite National Park and pushed the standards of aid climbing and free climbing.

As the sport of rock climbing matured and standards of difficulty rose, oddly the length of the cutting-edge climbs gradually shortened. In the 1960s the big routes were the multiday wall climbs, and free-climbing standards played a secondary role. But over time, more and more climbers focused on doing harder and harder free routes, then harder and harder individual moves. By the early 1980s the most famous climbs were usually short, single-pitch free climbs of fierce difficulty. Later in the '80s, rock climbing became even more focused on doing hard moves, to the extent that the traditional placement of protection while leading began to be replaced with fixed protection. "Sport climbing" allowed climbers to focus specifically on the gymnastic skills and strength necessary to make the hardest moves possible without worrying about the risk or energy drain required when placing protection.

The advent of sport climbing and its quick acceptance as a legitimate form of rock climbing changed the sport forever and made indoor climbing inevitable. The trend took off faster in Europe than in the United States, and for the first time in decades the best climbers were not Americans. Europeans, with their cable cars and espresso bars in their mountain huts, took bolted routes to their small crags with vigor. It was so convenient. Sport climbers committed to only single-pitch climbs. No hardware, other than carabiners and slings, was needed, and the protection and anchors were always in place. Climbers no longer needed to know much about how to place protection, build anchors and safety systems, or get themselves out of trouble.

A pair of shoes, a harness, a rope, a belay device, quickdraws, and a chalk bag were all the tools needed, and belaying was the only skill needed, to go out and rock climb. By the late '80s, sport climbing took off in America as well. Once that stage was reached, it was not long before the last variable—the environment—also came under the climber's control and the first indoor walls were built. Now climbers could learn and train without concern about any objective hazards in a climate controlled by a thermostat.

The first indoor walls were crude by today's standards, and they were initially scoffed at by the hard-core traditionalists as poor substitutes for the real thing. But, always inventive, climbers continued to build better and better mousetraps, and by the late 1990s the state of the art in climbing walls provided a high-quality medium; even the scoffers were frequently seen pumping plastic. What was once viewed as a fringe sport became mainstream, and everyone seemed to be climbing.

Indoor climbing is not rock climbing, but it is here to stay. For more and more climbers, the first handhold they grab will be one made in a factory. They will learn some of the fundamentals of the sport, build skill and confidence, and then decide to head outside. Thus rock climbing will have come full circle: from a part of mountaineering, to a specialty sport all its own, to artificial gymnastics done indoors, and, finally, to a venue through which initiates can learn the basics and then head back out to the mountains.

A NOTE ABOUT SAFETY

Safety is an important concern in all outdoor activities. No book can alert you to every hazard or anticipate the limitations of every reader. The descriptions of techniques and procedures in this book are intended to provide general information. This is not a complete text on climbing technique. Nothing substitutes for formal instruction, routine practice, and plenty of experience. When you follow any of the procedures described here, you assume responsibility for your own safety. Use this book as a general guide to further information. Under normal conditions, excursions into the backcountry require attention to traffic, road and trail conditions, weather, terrain, the capabilities of your party, and other factors. Keeping informed on current conditions and exercising common sense are the keys to a safe, enjoyable outing.

The Mountaineers Books

CHAPTER 1

Indoor Climbing—The Fundamentals

EQUIPMENT

Climbing is one of the most equipment-intensive sports around. It is chock full of specialized equipment that is unique and essential. Even the casual weekend climber has a closet stuffed with ropes, packs, shoes, and hardware of all kinds. In other outdoor sports, the equipment is more straightforward: white-water boaters need a boat, paddle, personal flotation device, helmet, and a few other things; skiers need skis, boots, poles, and a lift ticket. But climbing is different—we need so many specialty widgets, thingamajigs, and gizmos, it is simply amazing.

Obsession with gear is a malady common to climbers and can reach dizzying proportions. Pat Ament, a cutting-edge climber in Colorado three decades ago, relates a story about climbing in the Front Range with the legendary Layton Kor in 1962, in *Climb* by Bob Godfrey and Dudley Chelton (Boulder, Colo.: Alpine House Publishing, 1977, page 114): "We'd go screaming down to Eldorado in Layton's old car. He'd look at me and say, 'Got the RURPs?'—'Gosh, Layton, no, I thought you had

'em.' Around we'd spin, bald tires squealing, and tear back to Boulder to get them." Yes, he said *RURPs*. Realized Ultimate Reality Pitons are about the size of a postage stamp. What other sport needs things like RURPs?

Obsessed or not, we all need the right gear. Whether you are climbing indoors in a gym or outdoors, sport or traditional style, the basic equipment described in this section is necessary, really.

Safety Dynamics of Climbing Equipment

Climbing safety equipment is designed to be far stronger than necessary. When used correctly, climbing equipment in good condition does not break. However, when it is damaged or used incorrectly, climbing equipment can fail. Understanding why the gear is strong and how to use it is important in building confidence and instilling safe habits. An international testing agency, the International Union of Mountaineering Associations (Union Internationale des Associations Alpines, UIAA), sets standards and tests strengths for certain types of climbing safety equipment, including ropes, carabiners, harnesses, and helmets. Though not all equipment is tested by the UIAA, its seal of approval is one tool the climber can use when making decisions about what gear to buy.

ROPE

The climbing rope is what the entire safety system hangs from. Without a rope, all the other hardware is useless. Ropes are precisely engineered tools that allow people to safely push their limits, so understanding what makes them work is important.

Construction and Dimensions: Ropes are made of continuous nylon fibers and are constructed with an internal core and external sheath. The core accounts for most of the strength of the rope, whereas the sheath is woven to protect the core by providing abrasion resistance. Single climbing ropes—those designed to be used with one strand between climbers—range from about 9 millimeters in diameter to more than 11 mm, and from 150 feet (45 m) to more than 220 feet (70 m) long. Other ropes of smaller diameters are designed to be used two strands at a time—the systems

for double ropes are not covered in this book. Some ropes are chemically treated to repel water, which is most important for ice climbing.

Strength Characteristics: Climbing ropes are strong because they stretch during a fall ("static" ropes, which do not stretch, are applicable in some limited climbing situations, but their use is not covered in this book). By stretching, they absorb force so that when the fall is over, the load left on the system is less than the breaking strength of any of the equipment and low enough so that it will not injure the climber. If climbing ropes did not stretch, climbing equipment would break and climbers would be hurt. When you buy a rope, it will have a tag on it with several numbers, often in unfamiliar units of measure. Do not worry; it is really quite simple. There are three important numbers:

Maximum impact force—expressed in units of force such as kilonewtons (kN). It means the maximum force that can ever be exerted by the falling climber on the rope—when the fall is over, this is the force that remains and must be held by the system and endured by the climber. The maximum impact force allowed by the UIAA is 2,680 pounds and is determined in its drop test (see the paragraph on UIAA test falls held, below). The lower the impact force number is, the more elastic the rope is, which makes for longer, but softer, falls. Most ropes have a maximum tensile strength of more than 5,000 pounds, so even under the most severe circumstances can only be stressed to about half their strength.

Static elongation—the stretch of the rope under a body-weight load of 176 pounds (80 kg) expressed as a percentage of length. The higher the number, the more the rope will stretch when used for top-roping and rappelling.

UIAA test falls held—the number of test falls held before failure. This is perhaps the most misunderstood number of all. A rope that is rated for eight UIAA falls does not have to be retired after you take the eighth leader fall. The number means that the rope held eight falls before failure in a laboratory test. The test fall involves dropping a 176-pound (80 kg) load 16.5 feet on 8.25 feet of rope with the rope running over an edge that simulates a carabiner. This short fall produces the highest impact force possible—there is plenty of air time to generate forces, and little rope in the system to absorb the shock. In addition, there are no knots to tighten, belayers to shift, or any other system adjustments that might mitigate the force. This test fall cannot be duplicated under normal climbing conditions. In the lab, the test fall is repeated over a short period of time until the rope fails. The rope is always stressed at the same place, and no time is given between falls for the rope to recover—a rope stretched in a fall will rebound if left without tension for a while. With each test fall, there is less elasticity left and the impact force rises; it eventually exceed the tensile strength of the rope and the rope breaks. The stress of these repeated falls never occurs in the real world. A climbing rope can hold dozens and dozens of lead falls and many more top-rope falls. Ropes are retired because their owners feel they are past the point of being trustworthy, not because they are no longer strong enough to hold falls.

FALL FACTORS

The International Union of Mountaineering Association's (UIAA) testing involves test falls. *Fall factors* are useful for comparing the relative forces of falls. A test fall produces high force in part because the fall factor is very high. The fall factor is based on a calculation that divides the length of rope in the system into the length of the fall: a 10-foot fall on 10 feet of rope produces a fall factor of 1. The highest fall factor possible is 2. If a climber climbs 10 feet above the belay in the middle of a sheer cliff and falls off, he or she will fall 20 feet on 10 feet of rope, and produce a fall factor of 2 (20 divided by 10). If that same climber climbs 90 feet, places solid protection, climbs 10 more feet, and falls, he or she will still fall 20 feet but on 100 feet of rope, producing a fall factor of 0.2 (20 divided by 100). Fall factors such as this produce much lower forces. A goal of any climber should be to take every precaution so that potential fall factors are kept as low as possible—place lots of protection, especially early in a lead.

The bottom line is that all ropes are designed to be more than strong enough. An undamaged rope can never be stressed enough to break while climbing. The most important numbers to look at when considering buying a rope are diameter and length. Once you have settled on that, then consider the ropes in that category and compare them. If your primary use will be top-roping, then a rope with lower elongation and higher impact force may be fine; if you expect a lot of leader falls, perhaps the opposite would be better. If you are going to be hard on your rope, go fatter. If minimizing rope weight is important, go thinner. Ask the staff at retail stores to help you sort out the differences and make the best choice.

Care: When using your climbing rope, keep it clear of sharp edges and avoid stepping on it, which can drive dirt through the sheath and cause core damage. Do not expose it to any liquid except water. Use a rope bag to protect the rope during transport in your car and keep it clean when it is on the ground. Keep the rope away from all types of acids—such as that found in car batteries—and jumper cables. Ropes should be stored in a cool, dark, dry place. Clean a rope by braiding it or putting it in a pillow case and washing it with mild, nonliquid detergents in a washing machine without any bleach. Some manufacturers make special detergents for cleaning ropes—check the manufacturer's tag for more information. Let the rope air dry. Always take a few minutes to check your rope before using it. Run your hand down the length of it, feeling for mushy spots, fuzzy spots, or any sheath damage. Do not gamble if you find a bad spot—particularly if the core can be seen through the sheath. Cut any badly damaged sections off. The remaining portion can be used as a short climbing rope or for building top-rope anchors. With proper use and care, a rope will last several years.

ROCK SHOES

Rock shoes are specifically designed for rock climbing. They feature special, sticky rubber on the sole and *rand* (a rubber strip that runs around the outside of the shoe just above the sole). This provides superior friction and grip. A tight fit is essential. Even though rock shoes may be initially uncomfortable, the snug fit is important for standing on tiny edges and the sensitivity required to place the foot on microscopic rugosities. A loose fit means your foot will be sloppy in the shoe, and that will make your shoe sloppy on the rock. Most people wear their climbing shoes one to two sizes smaller than their street shoes. Many models and styles are available; they can be broken into the two following categories based on construction and performance.

Board-lasted: Rock shoes built around a stiff midsole are called *board-lasted*. This means that the edging power of the shoes is provided by the rigid *last* (the internal structure on the bottom of the shoe). Board-lasted shoes make good all-around shoes because they work well for edging, friction, and cracks. Because they do not require a toe-numbingly tight fit for performance, board-lasted shoes are recommended for climbers who have not developed the foot strength or tolerance for the tighter-fitting slip-lasted versions. Board-lasted shoes are available as high-tops that furnish ankle protection and a bit of support, or are low cut to provide greater mobility. Board-lasted shoes are recommended as the first pair of rock shoes for a novice climber.

This selection represents the standard climbing shoe styles, from left: The La Sportiva Kaukulator is board-lasted, the Hot Chile Habenaro is slip-lasted, and the La Sportiva Mistral is a slipper with Velcro closures.

Slip-lasted: Rock shoes built around a socklike last that provides superior sensitivity and performance for steep face climbing are called *slip-lasted.* Edging power is determined by a tight fit that packs the foot onto the smallest of holds and the strength of the climber's feet. Slip-lasted shoes are available as slippers or laced versions. They require a degree of foot strength to be used effectively because they do not provide much support. Conversely, as a training tool, slip-lasted shoes are a very effective tool to build foot strength.

Any type of rock shoe requires a proper fit for top performance. Use rock shoes with bare feet or, at most, a thin sock. Board-lasted shoes ideally fit with the longest toe touching the front of the shoe and the toe box comfortably filled by the foot. Toes do not have to be buckled over in the shoe. Slip-lasted shoes do require a degree of toe buckling. Some high-performance slip-lasted shoes require a severe, toe-down fit. They can provide the highest degree of sensitivity and performance in certain situations. This type of shoe takes experience to appreciate and is not for everyone. Though a snug fit is important, remember that a pair of rock shoes are of no use at all if they are too painful to wear, so do not go overboard trying to downsize.

HELMET

Helmets save lives and should be considered an essential piece of equipment when climbing outdoors. They are not used in rock gyms (though it is not a bad idea), but they are included here because a helmet is an essential piece of all-around equipment. They protect the climber and belayer from injury caused by falling objects, and also offer some protection in case of a fall. Like the seat belt in your car, your climbing helmet is the single most important piece of safety equipment you can use. Years ago helmets were heavy, uncomfortable, and boring, but now helmets are so light, comfortable, and stylish that there is no excuse for not wearing one. After a while you will not even notice that it is on your head. Helmet use

Modern helmets are lightweight and functional.

has increased in recent years—just as it did in bicycling a decade ago; it is a good trend.

Helmet Safety Dynamics

Construction: Most helmets are made of either fiberglass or some kind of plastic. Plastic helmets are lighter. Helmets are designed to protect the climber from the impact of falling objects. Some also provide side impact protection when a climber falls. They all have a suspension that keeps the helmet off the climber's head and are held on the climber's head by a chin strap.

Strength Characteristics: Climbing helmets are designed to absorb impact but they are not magic. They cannot protect the climber from big rocks, chunks of ice, or long, hard falls.

Care: Check regularly for cracking or delaminating. Fiberglass helmets last longer, up to fifteen years if not damaged. Because they break down chemically when exposed to ultraviolet (UV) light, plastic helmets have a shorter life span, about five years.

HARNESS

A harness consists of a waist belt, leg loops, a buckle, and, generally, a belay loop. There are three basic styles: alpine, fixed leg loops, and adjustable. Harnesses of all types come with gear loops attached to the waist belt.

Alpine or diaper-style harnesses do not have any leg loops to step through, so they can be put on while you are wearing skis or crampons. The leg loops are formed after the waist belt has been secured by pulling straps up and around the thighs. They are great for longer climbs on which the ability to drop the leg loops may be important. They also fit over a wide variety of clothing, so are great for summer rock climbing as well as winter climbing.

Harnesses with fixed leg loops are the most popular for rock climbing. They fit precisely over the clothes worn for rock climbing, usually have padded waist belts, and are the lightest and most comfortable harnesses. They do not adjust, however, so they will

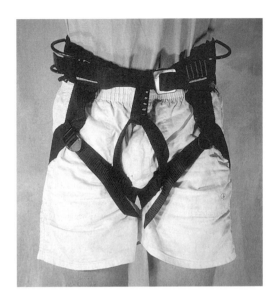

The alpine style harness forms leg loops by pulling straps up and around the thighs. These harnesses are sized extra small to extra large and each size has room for quite a bit of adjustment.

Harnesses with permanently sewn leg loops are very comfortable but they must be fitted correctly because they are not adjustable.

probably not fit over all the clothing needed for winter climbing.

Adjustable harnesses have buckles on the leg loops as well as the waist belt, so they will fit over just about anything. They are a little heavier than harnesses with fixed leg loops and usually not as comfortable, but the advantage of adjustability often outweighs these disadvantages.

Once the style of harness has been selected, work to get the right fit. Choose a harness primarily on fit. The thigh diameter, waist size, and *rise* (the vertical dimension between the leg loops and waist) all must combine to fit your individual requirements. On alpine and adjustable harnesses, the only decision is to buy one with the proper size of waist belt. When the harness is properly sized, there is

still some room on either side of the buckle to either tighten or loosen it. If you choose an adjustable harness that is too small, it may not buckle safely over winter clothing; if it is too large, it may not cinch down enough over a pair of shorts. On harnesses with fixed leg loops, be certain to fit the harness over the clothing you will be wearing when you climb. The waist belt should tighten in the middle of its adjustment range, and the leg loops should be snug around the upper thighs without restricting movement. The waist belt on any style of harness should be tightened enough so that it cannot be pulled down over the climber's hips.

When you try a harness on, hang in it off a rope, just as you will really be using it. Whatever the choice in harness, use it according

Adjustable harnesses have an adjustable waist belt and adjustable leg loops. They come is several sizes and there is great room for adjustment in each size.

to the manufacturer's directions. Pay close attention especially to the proper use of the buckling systems and tie-in locations.

Harness Safety Dynamics

Construction: Harnesses are made of nylon webbing of various widths, and may be padded or not.

Strength Characteristics: Harnesses are designed to hold the force of the most severe fall with ease. However, they are only strong enough when they are sized correctly and their buckles are threaded according to the manufacturer's specifications. Harnesses do not fail because they are not strong enough, but because they are not used properly.

Care: Check harnesses regularly for wear or damage. With proper care, most harnesses will last several years—check the manufacturer's recommendations.

BELAY/RAPPEL DEVICE

Every climber should have his or her own belay/rappel device. Important factors to consider in selecting these devices include braking power, ease of rope handling, versatility, and security.

Most belay/rappel devices work by creating a bend (or *bight*) in the rope that produces a manageable level of friction. A bight of rope is pushed through an opening slot and is then clipped into a locking carabiner (see section below). Braking and holding power is achieved by the choking action of the device pulled against the locking carabiner. Rope is handled through this type of device by specific techniques described in the belaying section later in this chapter.

The devices come shaped as plates or tubes. They work for both belaying and rappelling with either double or single ropes. There are also autolocking devices, which clamp the rope automatically when loaded. The Petzl Gri Gri is the only autolocking device discussed in this book. It is much heavier and more expensive than plate- or tube-style devices, but it does work beautifully. It can only be used for single-rope belaying or rappelling.

Figure-eight devices are for rappelling with either double or single ropes. They offer smooth rappelling, but can twist the ropes. Figure eights are limited in their use as a belay device. Check the manufacturer's recommendations.

CARABINERS

Carabiners are the metal snap links that connect the parts of the climbing system. Climbing carabiners are made of aluminum

Belay and rappel devices come in many styles. Shown here are plate and tube styles along with the self-locking Gri Gri and that old standby, the figure eight.

and come in two gate shapes: straight and bent. **Straight-gate carabiners** are the most versatile. They can be used for any application. **Bent-gate carabiners** have a dogleg in the gate that facilitates clipping the rope. For this function, they work very well. Bent-gate carabiners are to be used only on the rope-end of a sling or quickdraw. The bend in these carabiners that makes them easy to clip also makes it easy for them to unclip themselves. Bent-gates can unclip themselves if clipped directly to a fixed, immobile point like a bolt or piton. Be careful where they are used. **Wire-gate carabiners** are also available. Using wire instead of aluminum stock for the gate creates a carabiner with a huge gate opening, high strength, and great performance in freezing conditions (regular carabiners can freeze shut).

Wire-gate carabiners also minimize the phenomenon of gate flutter.

Laboratory tests have shown that during a high-force leader fall, the climbing rope moves rapidly through the protection-point carabiner. That action creates a harmonic vibration in the carabiner that can make the gate of the carabiner begin to open and shut very rapidly. This is called *gate flutter* and is amplified by the mass of the regular, aluminum-stock gate. It is possible, therefore, that the gate of the carabiner could be open when the load of the fall is caught by the carabiner. Carabiners are only about one-third as strong with the gate open as when it is shut. Carabiners do break; gate flutter, combined with a worn-out rope that is not absorbing enough energy, are two contributing factors. Another way to avoid this

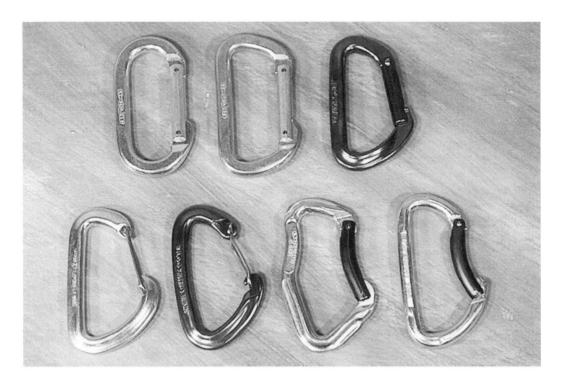

Non-locking carabiners come in a dizzying array of shapes and styles: standard ovals and D's, wire-gates, and bent-gates. Stick to the basics for a traditional rack and save the fancy ones for sport climbing.

situation, besides using wire-gate carabiners, is using lots of protection and locking carabiners (see section below) on potential high-force protection points.

Carabiners also are made in a variety of body styles. The most versatile is the D or modified D shape. They are strong and easy to use. Oval-shaped carabiners are good for racking, but not as strong, and sometimes it is hard to figure out where the gate opening is in a pinch.

There are some important numbers embossed on the spine of carabiners. They are the UIAA strength ratings. Carabiners are rated for failure strength with the gate closed in both the major (end-to-end) and minor (side-to-side) axes. High numbers are a good sign of a secure and durable carabiner, but sometimes at a premium price. Carabiners are rated in kilonewtons (kN), a measure of force, which is mass times acceleration. Remember, a falling climber is accelerating. For conversion purposes, 1 kN is approximately equal to the force of 220 pounds.

Locking carabiners are important, too. Besides the pear-shaped locking carabiner used on the harness as described in the previous section, it wise to have a couple more locking carabiners on the rack (the climber's collection of protection, slings, and other hardware) for other purposes. When in doubt, use a locking carabiner (see the next section).

Carabiner Safety Dynamics

Construction: Carabiners are made of aluminum and come in many shapes and styles. The basic shapes are oval, D, and bent-gate. The two basic styles of carabiner are nonlocking and locking. Nonlocking carabiners are used in most parts of the system between belays: They connect quickdraws and slings to pieces of protection, and are used to link parts of the belay anchor. Locking carabiners have a mechanism that locks their gates in the closed position. There are many variations that incorporate a screw gate or some kind of twisting lock mechanism. They are used when maximum security is needed: belaying, rappelling, clipping into an anchor, or creating a top-rope anchor.

Strength Characteristics: Carabiners are capable of holding far more than they will ever need to. However, they are only strong enough when they are loaded along their major axis and with the gate closed. Cross-loading them (along the minor axis) or loading them with their gate open greatly increases the risk of failure. When climbing, ensure that no carabiner will be cross-loaded, bent over an edge, or positioned in such a way that it could accidentally open.

Care: Carabiners need no special care. Keep them clean and check them periodically for excess wear (grooves worn from rappelling or lowering, weakened gate springs, cracks, et cetera). A carabiner that has been dropped a few feet but has no visible cracks can be put back into service.

LOCKING CARABINER

A locking carabiner is an essential part of your personal climbing gear. It attaches a belay/

rappel device to the harness, and is often used to attach the climber's rope to a belay anchor. A good choice for the primary locking carabiner is one that is large, easy to handle, and pear-shaped (called HMS). These carabiners do everything well, including operating a Munter hitch, a special belaying hitch described in the Knots section later in this chapter.

These carabiners all have locking mechanisms that help keep the gate closed and provide a much greater margin of safety over nonlocking carabiners. The lock on these carabiners consists of either a sleeve that screws over the gate or some type of spring-loaded autolocking mechanism. Either type works well, although screw-gate lockers can offer more security.

SLINGS AND QUICKDRAWS

Slings, or runners, are another essential part of the gear list. A sling is a loop of webbing ranging in length from 6 inches to 48 inches. Two feet is a standard length that can be easily carried over the shoulder. Slings have a number of uses, including hitching around trees and rock spikes for protection, extending shorter slings to reduce rope drag, and creating anchors. Always have about six standard-size slings available. Stitched slings are stronger and less bulky than hand-tied, knotted slings. Have some knotted slings available, however. It is handy to be able to untie a sling and thread it through an anchor point or around a tree to create a rappel anchor.

Shorter slings (4 to 6 inches) with a carabiner at each end are called *quickdraws*. A quickdraw is used as a connection between protection and the rope. Quickdraws are an essential piece of gear for sport climbing. A straight-gate carabiner is attached to one end

Locking carabiners come in various shapes and sizes and utilize several types of locking mechanisms. Pear-shaped lockers (called HMS) work well with a Munter hitch.

of the quickdraw and a bent-gate carabiner to the other end. The leader clips the straight-gate carabiner into a protection point and then clips the climbing rope into the bent-gate carabiner. Quickdraws can also be used for establishing top-rope belay anchors; they also work well for traditional climbs that follow a straight line. Shorter quickdraws that are stitched together tightly are easy to handle and work well for short, direct routes. A rubber gasket or stitched pocket holds the bent-gate, rope-end carabiner in place. Most sport routes require six to fifteen quickdraws.

Webbing and Cord Safety Dynamics

Construction and Dimensions: Webbing and cord are made of several different materials, including nylon, Spectra, and Kevlar. Webbing comes in widths from $1/2$ inch to 2 inches, and is woven either flat or tubular. One-inch, $9/16$-inch, and $11/16$-inch tubular webbing is used most often. Wider widths are great for tying off trees for belay anchors. The thinner widths are usually carried as permanent loops from 4 inches to 48 inches, and are used to make many connections in the climbing systems. Spectra webbing is stronger and more durable than nylon. Webbing comes presewn into loops; sewn webbing is incredibly strong. Or it can be purchased off the spool and cut to any length desired. Webbing bought off the spool has to be tied together using a water knot (see Knots section later in this chapter). Cord comes in sizes ranging from 3 mm to 9 mm and is most often used to make small permanent loops that will be used with clamping hitches, or tied in larger loops for *cordelettes* used in anchors and rescue systems. Cord is bought by the foot, and loops are tied using a triple fisherman knot (see Knots section later in this chapter).

Strength Characteristics: Webbing is static—it does not stretch—and in the standard widths of $9/16$ inch or larger has a breaking strength that greatly exceeds the maximum impact force the system could be subjected to. The strength of

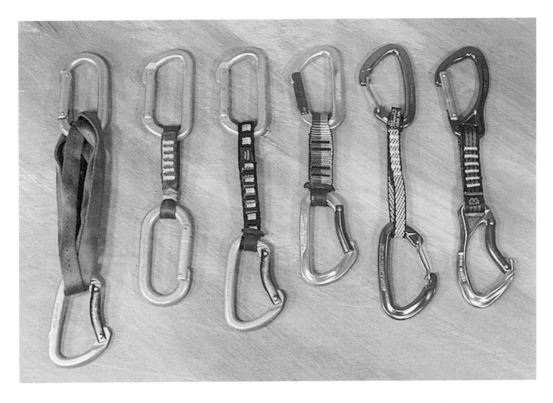

Quickdraws range from homemade with slings and carabiners, to component systems where you choose the carabiners and short, sewn slings, to fully assembled systems with specialty carabiners.

cord is dependent on the diameter and material—check the specifications before you buy it.

Care: Webbing and cord wear out from abrasion and with age. Visually check all webbing and cord regularly for excess wear or damage. Most climbers replace their slings and cords every couple of seasons.

CLOTHING

For climbing, dress in layers. Clothing for the gym climber is simple: shorts, sweats, tights, anything that is easy to move in. Gyms are often cold, so a sweatshirt or sweater is nice to wear until you are warmed up. Remember that you will be wearing a harness and that it is best to keep your waist area neat and visible. Superbaggy clothes or large shirts that cover up the harness are not recommended. Tuck shirts in and clothing under the harness, if possible.

Clothing for outdoor sport climbing is similar, but add a jacket and hat for weather protection. Sport climbing outside is characterized by periods of intense climbing that generates plenty of warmth, followed by long periods of standing around belaying or resting. Be prepared to pull on a jacket or even warm-up pants to stay warm in between climbs.

Longer traditional (trad) climbs require

more specialized clothing. It is entirely possible to be caught in changeable, severe weather high on a climbing route. An hour of cold rain can turn a pleasant outing into a survival epic. Choose synthetics for clothing on longer trad climbs because they do not absorb water, are warm when wet, and dry quickly. Always have a rain parka and possibly rain pants, a hat, and an extra warm vest or sweater accessible in a pack if the forecast is questionable.

CHALK

A chalk bag is a pouch filled with gymnastic chalk. It is worn on a belt around the climber's waist, where a hand can easily be dipped into it. Chalk dries the skin, which creates a better grip. Most people appreciate the benefits of chalk. Chalk helps a lot indoors, where the nature of the plastic holds, combined with high use, can produce some slippery holds. The act of chalking up is also a relaxation tool. Letting go, with one hand hanging, in the middle of a steep pitch requires control and poise. Chalking offers a chance to rest and strategize or to procrastinate if the next moves look scary.

Chalking up is also potentially a big mess. The fine white powder has a way of getting everywhere. Although a crumbled block of gymnastic chalk provides the best chalking performance, use some sort of enclosed chalk ball whenever possible. Chalk balls prevent messy spills when a chalk bag tips over and, more importantly, they help keep the air reasonably clear in a stuffy rock gym.

PACK

A small pack is ideal for carrying your equipment, extra clothing, and food and water. There are many brands and styles available, and the choices can be dizzying. Size and intended use are the two most important factors to consider, and will help you narrow the list of choices. A pack designed for climbing, with a volume of about 3,000 cubic inches, is appropriate for many climbs.

FOOD AND WATER

Rock climbing of any type requires lots of energy. Water is especially critical. In warmer weather, it is easy to drink more than two quarts of water per person each day. It is not unusual to see experienced climbers carrying a gallon water bottle with them for a day at the crag. On long multipitch routes, it is difficult to carry enough water. Even working out at the gym requires water. Always bring water.

Energy bars, chocolate, bagels, and fruit are the staples of a climber's lunch. Always have some food with you to maintain your energy level. An energy bar in your pocket makes a long climb much more comfortable.

KNOTS

Knots are central to climbing systems. They join everything—from the cord tied on your cams (a category of protective devices) to the rope tied on your waist—and they help to create belaying and self-rescue systems. In a sport as complex as rock climbing, you might expect that you would have to master many dozen different specialized knots, yet nearly the opposite is true. If you learn just a few knots and their variations, you can have a long and successful climbing career. While there are a host of other knots available, many of which serve purposes similar to the ones described here, this book describes only the most fundamental knots and their variations. The uses of each knot are described; tying instructions are given in the

A bight of rope, a loop, and a knot tied on a bight with a short tail showing.

form of illustrations. A few terms are useful as you learn these knots.

live end: the end of the rope being used, the end you are holding in your hand

standing end: the part of the rope running toward the far end; if you are tying into the rope, the live end is the end you are tying into and the standing end is the end of the rope that lies in a pile at your feet

bight: a pinched bend in the rope; the strands do not cross

loop: a bend in which the strands cross

tail: the live end of rope left over after tying a knot, and sticking out of the knot

on a bight: a knot formed in the middle of a rope

hitch: a wrapped connection around something—hitches do not stand on their own like knots; they fall apart if the thing they are hitched to is removed

dressing: the act of making a knot neat and tight

The knots that are described in this book are: figure eight follow-through, figure eight on a bight, double fisherman (half for a backup knot, triple for cordelettes), overhand on a bight, water knot, and mule knot. The hitches that are described in this book are: Munter hitch, girth hitch, clove hitch, and prusik/Klemheist/autoblock clamping hitches.

FIGURE EIGHT FOLLOW-THROUGH

This is the knot that creates the essential link between the climbing rope and the climber. It is strong and easy to identify, and it stays tied once it is tightened. It can also be tied around objects such as trees to anchor a rope for a belay anchor, and can be used to tie rope ends together. Though very secure, the figure eight follow-through is usually backed up with half of a double fisherman knot.

FIGURE EIGHT ON A BIGHT

This is the same knot as the figure eight follow-through, above, but is tied on a bight instead of

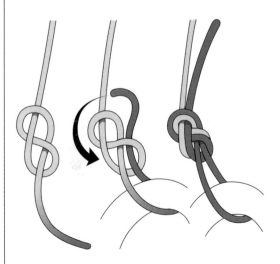

The figure eight follow through is the standard tie-in.

tracing in reverse back through the knot as in the figure eight follow-through. It forms a very strong and reliable loop, and is most often used as the master point in a belay anchor or to form the tether for a climber to clip into a belay anchor with.

DOUBLE FISHERMAN

This is the standard way to connect two ropes together. It consists of two knots tied around the rope that pull in opposition to each other and lock up. Half of this knot is used to back up a figure eight follow-through, and it is easy to tie on the end of a rope as a stopper knot to protect rappels. Used with three loops, it becomes a

triple fisherman, which is the standard way of tying cordelettes, the cord that runs through protection, or anything tied with Spectra or Kevlar cord.

OVERHAND ON A BIGHT

This is the simplest way of making a strong loop in a rope, a piece of cord, or webbing. When weighted, overhand loops are really hard to get out, so the knot is not recommended for high-load situations.

WATER KNOT

Also called the ring bend, this is a simple, retraced (like the figure eight on a bight, above)

The figure eight on a bight is used to clip to the belay anchor and has many other uses.

The double fisherman is a standard knot for tying two ropes together.

The overhand on a bight is the easiest way to make a strong loop.

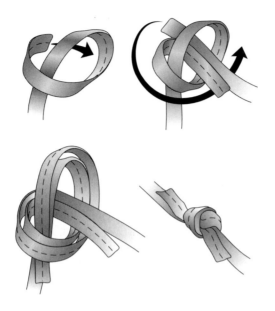

The water knot is the standard knot used to tie webbing together.

Tying the mule knot, step one: Form two loops as shown.

overhand knot that is tied in webbing to tie the ends of slings together. It must be tied very tightly, at least 2 inches of tail should be left, and the knot should be checked regularly because there is a tendency for the tails to creep toward the knot.

MULE KNOT

The mule knot is a type of slip knot tied around a rope or cord. It forms a blocking knot that will jam yet can be released easily, even while loaded. It figures prominently in belay escapes and other rescue situations.

MUNTER HITCH

The Munter hitch (see page 34) is a sliding hitch that allows you to control rope or cord being run through a belay. It is used for belaying and in many rescue situations. It is easy to feed rope in and out of a Munter hitch, and when weighted the hitch "flips" and locks. It can also be used for rappelling, although it tends to twist the rope dramatically in this application and is awkward and complicated to use on double ropes. If you know the Munter hitch, you need never worry again about dropping your belay device. This hitch works best on HMS carabiners.

GIRTH HITCH

The girth hitch is a fast and secure way to connect many things. It is the easiest way to link slings, secure a sling around a tree, or tie off a piton close to the rock.

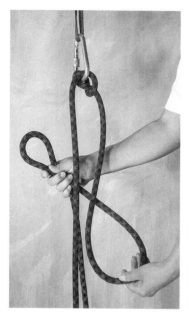

Step two: Pass the upper loop around the rope.

Step three: Pass the upper loop through the lower loop.

Step four: Tighten the knot, leaving a long tail-loop; for added security, tie the tail-loop around the loaded strand with an overhand knot.

CLOVE HITCH

The clove hitch is a marvelously useful knot. It can be used in place of a figure eight on a bight to connect a climber to the anchor, and is great for putting tension in a system, as when connecting nuts in opposition. The clove hitch is quick and easy to tie, and is easily adjustable once tied. It must be tied neatly or it can slip. The clove hitch is not as strong as other knots and should not be used in high-load situations.

PRUSIK/KLEMHEIST/AUTOBLOCK

These three clamping hitches are grouped together because they perform the same basic function—they are all used to attach cord or webbing directly to the rope, so that it can be loaded and then unloaded and slid along the rope. When weighted, these hitches bite into the rope and lock. When unweighted, they can be loosened and repositioned.

The prusik is a variation on the girth hitch, is very secure, and can be loaded in any direction, but it can be difficult to untie after a heavy load. It is the standard clamping hitch for rescue situations, and was used before mechanical ascenders were invented for ascending a rope.

The Klemheist hitch provides slightly less holding power than the prusik, should only be

The Munter hitch is a sliding hitch with many uses.

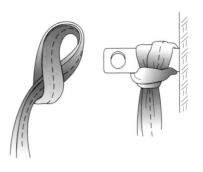

The girth hitch is an efficient way to tie off a partially driven piton.

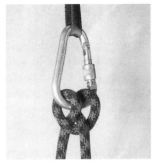

The clove hitch is a moderately strong, easily adjustable knot.

The prusik is a hitch consisting of multiple girth hitches; the more wraps, the greater the holding power. It can be loaded in any direction.

The Klemheist hitch is easy to attach to the rope and is perhaps the best all-around clamping hitch. For maximum holding power, it must be put on the rope so the load strand makes a sharp bend through the small loop.

The autoblock has the least holding power of the clamping hitches. It is very easy to take on and off the rope—simply wrap the sling around the rope several times and clip the ends together. The autoblock is great as a self-belay for backing up a rappel.

loaded in one direction (holding power is greatly reduced when loaded the other way), and releases easily after being loaded.

The autoblock hitch provides the least holding power of the three clamping hitches but is nonetheless sufficiently strong enough for low-load situations like backing up a rappel.

SIGNALS

Proper and clear communication is another key to safe climbing. Communication between belayer and climber can be difficult. Whether you are in a crowded gym or on a windy crag, sometimes it is impossible to hear exactly what the climber 50 feet above you said. The following commands are standard for all types of climbing and should be used at all times. These standard commands provide not only the words, but the syntax, that make communication possible in difficult situations.

"On Belay"—given by the belayer; means the belay is in effect, a fall will be caught from that point on, the climber may begin climbing.

"Belay On"—given by the climber; confirms that the belay is on.

"Climbing"—given by the climber; tells the belayer that the climber is starting to climb.

"Climb Away"—given by the belayer; tells the climber that the belayer knows the partner is climbing. Do not climb until you hear this; it is confirmation that the belayer is paying attention. Climbers have been hurt falling in the first few feet of a climb because the belayer was not aware the climber had started.

"Slack"—given by the climber; requested when the rope is too tight. This command can be confusing. If the climber yells, "Take up the slack" because he or she wants the rope tighter, the belayer may only hear "Slack" and give the

climber the opposite of what he or she wants. Then the climber will probably yell, "Take up the slack" even louder! Be sure to get this signal straight before starting.

"Up Rope"—given by the climber; means that too much slack has developed and the climber wants the belayer to take it in. This is what you yell instead of "Take up the slack."

"Tension"—given by the climber; means the climber wants a very tight rope to feel secure.

"Watch Me"—given by the climber; signals the belayer that the climber is at a tough move and thinks he or she may fall.

"Falling"—given by the climber; means the climber is actually falling or, just as likely, thinks he or she is about to fall—when climbers are really falling, they usually yell "Aaahh!"

"Take"—given by the climber; means almost the same as "Falling" but is more controlled and actually means that the climber intends to fall. It is a sport-climbing term that means "I'm letting go, please lock off the belay." The climber may shout "Take" when he or she has clipped into the top anchor or cannot make a move and plans to take a short (less than 5 feet) lead fall. "Take" is not often used on poorly protected traditional routes.

"On Rappel"—given by the climber; tells others that the climber is about to rappel, and alerts those giving a fireman's belay.

"Off Belay"—given by the climber; tells the belayer that the climber is anchored or on the ground and that the climber no longer needs the protection of the belay.

"Belay Off"—given by the belayer; tells the climber that the rope is out of the belay device.

"Off Rappel"—given by the climber; means the rappeller is no longer attached to the rope and is anchored or on the ground.

"Rope"—given by the climber; when yelled from above, tells others that rope is about to be dropped. If at a crowded area, the climber should wait to hear "Clear" before tossing the rope.

"Clear"—given by the belayer or those on the ground; is an answer to "Rope" and means the area is clear, it is OK to drop the rope.

"Rock"—given by anyone; means something is coming down, look out—should be yelled by anyone who sees something falling.

RATINGS

Climbers love talking not only about gear, but also about numbers. All climbs get rated using one or more grading systems, and climbers just cannot seem to talk about their climbs without tossing the numbers around. Rarely do you hear a climber back from the crag say, "It was a beautiful climb with interesting moves, wonderful positions, and long sections of exhilarating face climbing. I found it just within my limits." You are more likely to hear, "It was eight pitches, mostly 5.7 with some 5.9 sections, a strenuous 10b crux of inch-and-a-quarter hands, and a short section of A2 that I think would go at 12c. It's definitely not Grade III, there're too many pitches under 5.8, but it should get an R rating for the crux pitch, which fortunately was well below my level. Oh, and did I mention I on-sight 11c, redpoint 12b, have worked all the moves on a 12d, and last week climbed a V7?" Yes, climbers love their numbers. It is a way of comparing one climb to another—and one climber to another. Most other countries around the world that have a significant climbing history and tradition have their own rating systems. In the United States, all rock climbs are rated according to:

Grade—a commitment rating that tells how long it should take a competent party to complete the route.

Class—a general difficulty rating that ranges from hiking and scrambling to free climbing and aid climbing. Many different systems have evolved to measure technical difficulty.

Seriousness—a three-point scale that describes how well a free climb is protected.

Bouldering—a rating system for boulder problems that takes into account only the sheer difficulty of the moves.

GRADE (COMMITMENT)

Roman numerals I through VII measure the commitment of the climb, its overall nature, and, specifically, how much time it will take. The fictitious "average climber" is used to figure the time. Expert climbers can speed up a route in a few hours that could take less-talented climbers days to complete. The grade rating only really applies to traditional climbing. Sport climbs are generally one-pitch routes that are easily accessible; they are not referred to as Grade I. Multipitch climbs are where the grade rating is applied:

Grade I: 1 to 3 hours.

Grade II: 2 to 4 hours.

Grade III: 4 to 6 hours. Most of a day.

Grade IV: 1 full day.

Grade V: 1 or 2 days. Most parties will bivouac.

Grade VI: Several days.

Grade VII: Many days, combined with extreme difficulties, length, and exposed, alpine positions.

Remember, expert climbers have completed more than one Grade VI in a single day in Yosemite National Park, so the grade rating is relative to your experience, fitness, familiarity with the route, and motivation.

CLASS (DIFFICULTY)

Rating the technical difficulty of a climb is a tricky thing to do. Many factors contribute to the difficulty of a climb, and each climber experiences the climb slightly differently. Class ratings are, therefore, based on the consensus of many climbers who are experienced at climbing in many different areas. Ideally a route with a certain rating in the Shawangunks in New York state will feel as hard as a climb with the same rating in Joshua Tree National Park in California. Climbing is broken into the six following classes:

Class 1: Walking on easy terrain—most hiking trails.

Class 2: Rugged, often steep, rough trails.

Class 3: Easy scrambling that uses occasional hand- and footholds but does not require the use of a rope, even for a beginner. A slip on Class 3 terrain will not become a fall. To "third-class" a route means to climb it without a rope—many extremely difficult rock climbs have been soloed this way, but climbers take the ultimate risk in doing so.

Class 4: Easy climbing, but with enough exposure to warrant a rope and belay. A slip could become a fall. Intermediate protection points are used sparingly. Climbers often move together.

Class 5: Difficult "free climbing" wherein each hand- and foothold is chosen specifically. Belays and intermediate protection are required. One climber moves at a time.

This rating is further subdivided into an open-ended scale of decimal fractions from 5.0 to 5.14; the categories of 5.10 (pronounced "five-ten") and above are then subdivided by the letters *a* through *d,* currently up to 5.14d. This system is referred to as the **Yosemite Decimal System** (YDS). Indoor climbing ratings are usually based on the YDS 5.0–5.14d scale, although the system is not consistently applied. Because of the positive nature of indoor holds, routes often feel easier than a similarly graded route outdoors. The YDS is used primarily in the United States. Most other countries with a significant climbing history and tradition have their own rating systems.

Class 6 (aid climbing): Hand- and footholds are no longer sufficient to make progress and the climber must use artificial assistance to move upward. Specialized equipment is needed. Today, aid climbing is rated A1 through A5—the higher the number, the less secure the protection placements are and the greater the risk of a long and dangerous fall.

SERIOUSNESS

Not all traditional climbs protect well—they do not always provide consistently solid protection. Guidebooks usually use "R" and "X" ratings to alert the potential leader of dangers. If a climb does not have a protection rating of R or X, it is assumed that it can be protected relatively safely by a competent leader.

If a climb has an **R rating,** it means that the protection is sparse, difficult to place, or insecure (for example, little nuts behind an expanding flake at the crux), and the leader risks a long fall and the possibility of injury. Before you step onto an R-rated climb, be sure you are mentally, physically, and technically prepared.

If a climb carries an **X rating,** it means that protection is lacking or of terrible quality, and a falling leader could be seriously or fatally injured. Do not take this rating lightly, especially if the difficulty rating is near your limit—leading an X-rated climb is akin to soloing, and you had better be prepared to take the risk.

UIAA	French	Yosemite Decimal System	Australian	Brazilian	British a.	British b.
I	1	5.2			3a	
II	2	5.3	11		3b	VD
III	3	5.4	12	II	3c	HVD
IV	4	5.5		IIsup	4a	MS / S / HS
V-		5.6	13	III	4b	
V	5	5.7	14	IIIsup		VS
V +			15		4c	
VI-		5.8	16	IV	5a	
VI	6a	5.9	17 / 18	IVsup	5a	HVS
VI +	6a +	5.10a	19	V	5b	E1
VII-	6b	5.10b	20	Vsup	5b	E2
VII	6b +	5.10c / 5.10d	21 / 22	VI / VIsup	5c	E3
VII +	6c / 6c +	5.11a / 5.11b	23	VII	6a	E4
VIII-	7a	5.11c	24	VIIsup	6a	
VIII	7a +	5.11d	25	VIII	6b	E5
VIII +	7b / 7b +	5.12a / 5.12b	26	VIIIsup	6c	
IX-	7c	5.12c	27		6c	E6
IX	7c +	5.12d / 5.13a	28		7a	E7
IX +	8a	5.13b	29			
X-	8a +	5.13c	30 / 31			
X	8b / 8b +	5.13d	32			
X +	8c	5.14a	33			
		5.14b				
		5.14c				
		5.14d				

BOULDERING

In the United States the "V" system is used to rate bouldering problems. It currently runs from V0 to V14. For comparison, a V0 is about 5.9, a V5 is about 5.12, and a V11 is 5.14.

FREQUENTLY USED MOVES

A climber is only as good as his or her grip on the rock. How to use handholds, footholds, and body-position techniques is key to being able to get up a route. When combined with strength, good balance, a sense of timing, and a relaxed attitude, even the smallest holds can work. This section gives a description of the most frequently used holds, with accompanying illustrations. On any given route, a host of holds and moves may be needed, so practice them all in the gym until you are prepared to "lunge" for the "pocket," pull into a "gaston," and then "stem" to the final "mantle."

HANDHOLDS

Crimp: A handhold position for a very small hold wherein the fingers are hyperextended (first knuckle flexed). Locking the thumb around the fingers increases power. This is the strongest way to hold small edges, but it is hard on the fingers. Taping the areas between the knuckles helps support the fingers and is recommended for sustained crimping. Grip with the pads of the fingers, not the tips or nails.

Open grip: A handhold grip wherein the fingers are not hyperextended but, rather, in a natural open position. This is the best hold for training because it is easy on the fingers. Large, sloping holds develop this type of grip strength.

Pinch: A handhold position, squeezing a vertical hold between thumb and fingers.

The crimp hold places maximum stress on fingers but also offers strength and security on small edges; taping the finger joints helps protect tendons.

The open grip is friendlier on the tendons and works well on large holds.

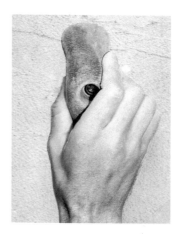

Pinch holds are rarely good enough to really pull on, but often provide a critical balance point for the next move.

Pockets range from single-finger, single-digit horrors to four-finger buckets.

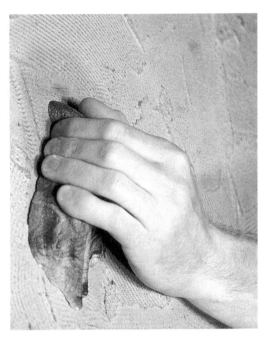

A side pull can be great for maintaining balance or can provide the essential leverage for a move upward.

Pocket: A handhold created by a hole. Pockets range in size from a single-finger pocket to one large enough for all four fingers. Try to keep your fingers in the open position when gripping pockets. Some climbers find that the middle and ring fingers are the strongest two fingers for a two-finger pocket. Hold your index and little fingers with your thumb on a two-finger pocket.

Side pull: A vertical handhold pulled on with the fingers, with the thumb up and the fingers aligned vertically and reaching away from the body.

Gaston: A vertical handhold like a side pull, but held with the thumb down and close to the body.

MOVES AND POSITIONS

Mantel: A series of moves to climb up onto a ledge. The climber pulls up on the ledge and then positions the arms under the body so he or she can push up onto straight arms, high-step (see below) up onto the ledge with a foot, then stand up. It is like getting out of a swimming pool, but is often easier said than done!

Undercling: A move that involves pulling up on a handhold, often a flake or incut edge, when the positive aspect of the hold faces down.

Lock-off: A position wherein the body is held in close to the wall off a handhold held tightly while the other hand reaches for the next hold.

Stemming: A move that involves applying counterpressure between two opposing surfaces; for example, in a corner, in a chimney, or between two large holds. Stemming is an excellent technique to learn for real rock climbing because it can provide a good resting position. Also called *bridging*.

Lieback: A crack climbing technique especially suited for offset corners. Arms pull on one side of the feature while the legs push against the opposite wall. Often strenuous.

Jamming: A crack climbing technique in which hands and feet are wedged into a crack for purchase. For more crack technique, see chapter 3, Traditional (Rock) Climbing.

Matching: Switching hands on a single hold.

Static: Accomplishing a move or series of moves in a very controlled and precise manner. Compare to *dynamic*.

Manteling involves a series of moves that are similar to the ones used to get out of a swimming pool.

An undercling is used when a handhold is upside down; it is particularly useful on steep walls or when climbing out overhangs.

The lock-off position allows you to reach for the next hold statically and in control; specific exercises will help you develop lock-off strength.

Above and upper right: Stemming on steep walls or corners, or in chimneys, helps keep the climber's weight on the feet instead of the arms.

Liebacking isn't just useful in cracks and corners; here a climber uses the positive edge of an arête to lieback upward.

Dynamic: Performing a move, or moves, with much movement, even a lunge-type surge. *Dyno* for short, as in "dyno for the ledge." An excellent technique for extreme climbing, but scary to perform when leading.

FOOTHOLDS

Edging: A foothold position wherein the foot is precisely held on the hold, generally on the inside area of the big toe. The angle of the foot to the wall should be about 45 degrees. Raise the heel for more precision, lower the heel to rest. This is the most common face-climbing foothold. You can also use the outside edge of the foot, around the little toe area, when backstepping.

Front pointing: A foot position wherein the foot is perpendicular to the climbing surface,

The inside edge is one of the strongest foot positions: Place the ball of your foot under your big toe on the hold, and keep your heels low and away from the rock. An outside edge can also be secure—especially if you have strong feet!

Dynamic moves require precision, timing, and confidence to be effective—miss the hold or fail to reach it and your next move will likely be out into space.

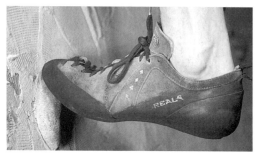

Front pointing is most useful on climbs with lots of pockets where conventional edging won't work because the edge is recessed.

and the very front of the shoe is edging. The heel is generally held high for maximum purchase. This foothold works well in pockets.

Smearing: A foot position wherein maximum sole area is applied to the rock. Generally, the toe is pointed up and the foot is flexed, heel low, allowing maximum contact of the sole of the shoe to grip the rock. Used for sloping holds, friction slabs, and liebacking, and anytime there is no feature to edge on.

Backstepping: A technique wherein the climber is sideways to the rock, with the hips perpendicular to the climbing surface. The climber backsteps and reaches with the arm on the rock side of the body. This works best on vertical and overhanging terrain.

Crunch: A position wherein the feet are brought up close to the hands. This is a strenuous position to hold because so much muscle flexing is required.

Rest position: A position wherein the climber hangs straight off an arm, using the skeletal system, not muscles, from which to hang the body.

Flagging: A technique to counterweight with a leg to maintain balance. Flag in by crossing one leg behind the other leg, or flag out by counterweighting with a leg to the side.

Highstep: A move wherein the climber steps very high to a foothold, rocks onto it with the body, then presses up with leg muscles to stand up. This is effective but tough on the knees.

Smearing depends on the friction between the sole of the shoe and the rock, and is used when there is no obvious foothold; keep the bottom of your shoes clean and your heels low.

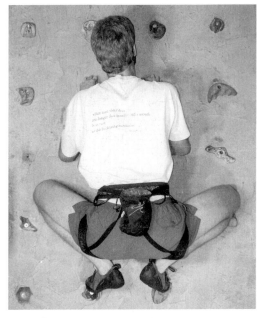

The crunch is a strenuous position to hold but sets the climber up well for a long reach; often the position from which a dynamic move will begin.

The rest position supports the body using the skeleton instead of the muscles.

Flagging uses the counterweight of a hanging leg to maintain balance and allow for a controlled reach. Here the climber flags his left foot behind his right allowing a long reach up and left.

The key to making a highstep is to transfer your weight over the high foot before pushing up on it.

BELAYING

You can have the gear, know your knots and signals, know the rating of the route, and have the moves memorized, but unless you can belay safely, you are not ready to climb. No other skill is as important to safe climbing than belaying, and there is no better compliment than to be described as a great belayer. Learn the techniques and responsibilities of belaying, and practice until it is second nature—remember, your partner is literally trusting you with his or her life.

The term *belay* is derived from a French verb that means "to hold fast." For the climber, to belay means to protect a climber by controlling his or her rope so that in the case of a fall, the rope will be held fast. The key to a good belay is friction. Belay devices provide manageable friction by putting a bend in the rope that allows the belayer to feed rope out and take rope in easily, yet lock off to catch a fall. Proper rope handling, communication, and technique are mandatory elements of safe belaying. The following elements of the belay system are universal to all types of climbing. Start by learning these techniques either in a gym or other controlled environment with an instructor.

SETTING UP A BELAY

After the climber is tied in, the belayer must set up a belay. Grasp the rope a comfortable distance from the climber and form a bight in the rope. Push the bight through the appropriate hole or slot in the belay device. Clip the bight into the locking carabiner that is clipped into the harness's belay loop (a vertically oriented, full-strength sewn loop on the front of many harnesses connecting the waist belt to the leg loops) or through the crotch strap and waist belt on harnesses without a belay loop.

The retaining cable of the belay device is also clipped into the locking carabiner. (Practice inserting and removing the rope from the belay device without ever removing the retaining cable from the locking carabiner; it is a habit that will help prevent dropping the device.) Lock the locking carabiner.

ROPE HANDLING

The first thing to do after the belay device is loaded is to identify the brake hand. The standing end of the rope—the part that emerges from the belay device and does not lead to the climber—is the brake side of the rope. The hand that holds that side of the rope is the *brake hand.* The hand on the live end of the rope—the end going to the climber—is called the *guide hand.* The number-one rule of belaying is to never let go with the brake hand. To stop a fall, or to hold a climber on the rope, pull back with the brake hand. This action bends the rope around the belay device, clamping the device against the locking carabiner. The friction that is created stops the fall. Braking is achieved by this technique. It is not a matter of a strong grip; the equipment does the job.

When the climber moves away from the belayer, slack must be fed out. This is done with each hand on its respective side of the rope, simultaneously feeding and pushing the rope out to the climber. The brake hand naturally stays on the rope during this motion.

Taking the rope in as a climber moves toward the belayer is a bit more difficult. Here are the best techniques: As the climber moves up and slack develops, pull the rope through the belay device with the brake hand. The guide hand can assist by pushing the rope into the device. When the brake hand is extended out a comfortable distance, slide the guide hand up the standing side of the rope until it is possible to pinch the brake side of the rope with the guide hand above the brake hand. Both sides of the rope are now momentarily held in the guide hand. This allows the brake hand to slide down the brake side of the rope toward the belay device without ever letting go of the braking side of the rope, and prevents any rope from slipping back through the belay device. The process is continually repeated as the climber progresses, and the belayer is always ready to lock the rope off in the brake position should a fall occur.

This is not an easy technique to learn. One trick is to start learning in "first gear." Keep the guide hand extended straight out, with both sides of the rope running through the open

Belaying method number one: The left hand is the guide hand and the right hand is the brake hand. The rope must be taken in without letting go of the brake hand.

Step one: Begin pulling rope through the belay device with the brake hand while leaving the guide hand out in front.

Step two: After a length of rope has been pulled through the device, open the guide hand and drop the brake strand into it. Keep your brake hand closer to your body so you do not have as far to move it in step three.

Step three: Pinch the two strands together in the guide hand and slide the brake hand back down the rope to the device. Repeat the steps to continue taking in rope.

palm. Pull rope through the device and toward the guide hand with the brake hand. Allow both ropes to easily slide through the guide hand until the moment when the two hands meet. Then quickly pinch the brake side of the rope with the guide hand and slide the brake hand back down the rope to prepare to pull in another length. Do not move the extended guide hand; just relax and let the rope run through it until it has to pinch the brake strand. As soon as this is mastered, move to "second gear." Now the guide hand starts moving back and forth in conjunction with the brake hand, pulling the rope in, then extending out to pinch the brake rope while the brake hand slides down. Practice!

Another method that works well is for the

Belaying method number two:

Step one: With the brake hand oriented so that the thumb is closer to the belay device, pull slack through the device with the brake hand, and then lock the belay device off by pulling back on the brake hand.

Step two: Reach back and hold the lock-off position with the guide hand then slide the brake hand back down to the belay device.

belayer to pull the rope through the device with the brake hand, lock the device off, reach over and hold the lock-off position with the guide hand, and then slide the brake hand back down.

LOWERING

The belayer often has the job of lowering the climber back down to the ground after the climber has reached the top of the climb. Lowering begins with proper communication—see the Signals section earlier in this chapter for a refresher. The belayer first pulls in as much slack as possible through the belay device until the climber is felt on the rope. Then the belayer locks off the rope in the brake position. The climber weights the rope and the belayer lowers the climber down. Allow the belay device to do the lowering by adjusting the angle of the brake side of the rope as it feeds into the device. The climber will lower faster as the rope is raised up, slower as it is angled more sharply down toward the brake position. Using both hands on the brake end of the rope makes for smooth lowering. Let the rope run through your hand at a moderately slow pace. Try not to be jerky. A pair of leather belay gloves make the process more comfortable on novice hands.

USING A PETZL GRI GRI

The Petzl Gri Gri, an auto-locking belay device that is quite popular, is the only auto-locking belay device included in this book. The Gri Gri works on a different principle from traditional devices. The rope is fed through the Gri Gri following the instructions on the device. Pulling in the slack ("up rope") is done with the same hand motions as with any other device. When a fall occurs or the climber weights the rope, the Gri Gri automatically grips the rope by a secure camming action. Even though the Gri Gri locks "automatically,"

it is still critical that the brake hand remain on the rope at all times. Lowering the climber with a Gri Gri is performed by raising the spring-loaded handle until the rope begins to run, assisted by friction from the brake hand. This is very different from lowering with a traditional belay device, and should be practiced diligently. If the belayer panics and pulls the lever too hard when lowering, the rope will fly through the device with almost no friction.

TRAINING

Climbing indoors or outdoors is a demanding physical activity that requires at least a minimum level of conditioning. A reasonably fit person can immediately enjoy his or her first experience climbing an easy route without any special training. Fingers and forearms may initially tire quickly from gripping the handholds, but the fun makes up for it. "Contact strength" is the limiting factor for all rock climbers, whether new or experienced. As a person's interest in climbing develops, it is natural to progress to longer and harder climbs. The best way to accomplish this is by some sort of training regimen.

Training for climbing does not necessarily mean strict schedules and documented sessions. It can be as simple as some common-sense approaches to using the rock gym and creating a lifestyle that helps avoid injury and promotes gradual muscular strength gains. In the past, climbers would get in shape for the climbing season by a training hike or two in the local hills, occasional pull-ups, and repeating the standard easy climbs at the crags. The existence of rock gyms have changed all that. Now it is possible to train full-time specifically for climbing. Climbing is no longer constrained by seasons; it is a year-round sport. Unfortunately, with this unlimited opportunity for improvement comes the threat of injury from too much training. Overuse injuries are the biggest hazard associated with rock gyms.

INJURY PREVENTION

Injuries at a rock gym rarely occur from falls or accidents. The most common injuries result from too much training and climbing. Almost everyone who climbs in a gym will suffer some sort of muscle or tendon injury at some point. Because of the steep and strenuous terrain, gym climbing puts a tremendous strain on fingers, elbows, and shoulders. These areas of the body are held together with connective tendons. Muscles develop roughly twice as fast as tendons, so it is not unusual for a gym climber to quickly get literally too strong for his or her own good. Following are some tips to avoid injury:

- Do not overdo it. Avoid overtraining. Tendonitis (inflammation of tendons) usually occurs because of too much climbing. No climber can crank hard every day without paying a price.
- Rest. Getting enough rest between gym sessions is as important as the training itself. A good rule of thumb is to never climb hard the day following a major pumpfest. Cross-train with other activities if you must do something.
- Be balanced. Mix endurance training with strength-building and technique exercises. Blend weight training and cross training. Evolve your schedule with the seasons.
- Use preemptive taping. Support the areas in your fingers between the joints with strips of tape to support the tendons before they get sore.

- Let go. Training at the gym is just that—training. If something hurts, let go and drop off!
- Avoid extreme moves. Highsteps, dynos, long reaches, tiny holds, and one-finger pockets are examples of moves that can hurt.
- Do not do things that hurt. If a certain type of move or terrain hurts, avoid it. For example, steep cave climbing can tax your shoulders. If you are prone to shoulder pain, avoid caves.
- Use soft holds. Some holds have sharp edges or cause your fingers to flex unnaturally. Look for hold that are "soft" and conform to your natural grip.
- Heed warning signs. If you wake up at night with a sore elbow, it is probably a sign not to climb the next day.

Bouldering caves are great for developing strength, but the workout sessions are strenuous, so do not overdo it; if it hurts, stop.

■ If it keeps hurting, see a doctor. A rule of thumb is if you are injured, rest until the pain goes away. Then, rest that time period again to ensure complete healing. If that does not work, see a professional.

AEROBIC TRAINING

Rock climbing is not a particularly demanding aerobic activity. Muscle failure in rock climbing is generally due to getting "pumped," the condition when forearm muscles fill with blood and retain lactic acid (a by-product of muscles working), then they cramp, swell, and refuse to operate. However, a certain level of aerobic fitness is certainly recommended for a rock climber. The approaches and descents from many climbs can be long and strenuous. It is not unusual to hike 2 or 3 miles steeply uphill to reach the base of a climb. Schlepping a heavy pack of gear, ropes, and water adds to the effort. Descents can be tedious, long walks or scrambles down difficult terrain. For reasons of both added enjoyment and safety, rock climbers need to be in decent aerobic shape.

A minimum aerobic program for climbers would involve a couple of half-hour sessions per week combined with weekend activities. Suggested exercises include 30 minutes of running, biking, fast walking, or any other activity that keeps the heart rate up. On the weekends (if you are not out climbing), go mountaineering, hiking, biking, cross-country skiing, or something similar. Probably the best advice is to create a lifestyle that includes different levels of aerobic activity that become a part of the day-to-day routine.

If your rock-climbing goals include bigger and more remote climbs that require long and steep walks in, then by all means step up your aerobic training accordingly. Increase the frequency and level of training runs or rides. Take advantage of every opportunity to simulate the aerobic activity that you are preparing for; that is, carrying a heavy pack up a steep hill. Yes, humping a pack up a hot trail can be boring and miserable work. Learn to pace yourself, stay refueled with water and snacks, and recover with rest breaks, and perhaps you will find it is not that bad. You may even find it perversely enjoyable.

WEIGHT TRAINING

The use of free weights can dramatically improve climbing performance, especially if you have never trained with weights before. Weight training can be effective for strengthening climbing-specific muscles and developing other muscle groups that can help prevent injury. For example, pull-ups were for years considered the primary training exercise for rock climbing. Climbers often did lots of pull-ups, and little else. The results were strong climbers, but also chronically sore elbows and shoulders from the repetitive and strenuous nature of the exercise. Balancing a climbing-specific movement like pull-ups with other exercises (for example, bench presses or push-ups) helps build opposing muscles groups that can prevent overuse injuries.

It is essential that anyone new to weight training or considering adding a weight-training regimen into his or her daily schedule gets more detailed and personalized information than can be offered here. There are many resources available, from books and periodicals to certified personal trainers at a local gym. One good reference is *Conditioning for Outdoor Fitness* by David Musnick and Mark Pierce (Seattle: The Mountaineers Books, 1999). Needless to say, incorrect training techniques can do more harm than good. Remember, too, that it takes time to develop the awareness of your personal style, learn how your muscles respond to specific exercises, and find out what works best for you. Gains do not come overnight.

Suggested weight-training exercises to build a basic training program include lat (latissimus dorsi) pulls, bench presses, squats, biceps curls, overhead presses, chest flys, and triceps pushdowns. Exercises that do not require special equipment include pull-ups, dips, sit-ups, and push-ups. Remember that some of these exercises (like pull-ups or dips) are very difficult and may require assistance to complete.

PERIODIZATION

A year-round training program ideally incorporates weight training, aerobic activities, climbing-specific exercises, and cross training. The quantity and intensity of training depends on the season. For example, winter is traditionally a time when rock climbers hit the gym to build a base of strength for the upcoming year with weight training. As spring approaches, the mix becomes more climbing-specific as actual climbing begins. Summer is a time of maintenance with light training and running between climbs. Fall is sometimes a great season for a climbing road trip, so training becomes more climbing-specific to help reach a goal.

For most climbers, training for rock climbing means doing lots of climbing. In many ways, this is the best approach, because nothing trains you for the real thing like the real thing. Outdoor rock climbing can be used as a vehicle for training, except that it rarely offers consistency. Weather can be poor, the climbing can be too easy or too hard, and too many factors are uncontrollable. Indoor

climbing, in a gym or on a home wall, has changed that by providing a controlled environment. Now a climber can plan exactly when and how a climbing-specific workout will occur. The result is that it is easier than ever to quickly learn how to climb well and get fiendishly strong. The downside is that it is also possible to overdo it way too quickly, and suffer chronic overuse injuries. To be effective and smart in a gym or other controlled climbing environment, approach the experience with a plan. Start with a warm-up, then focus on endurance or difficult climbing such as trying a hard redpoint.

WARMING UP

Warming up is the crucial first step. For a climber, the most important muscles to warm up are those in the forearms that control the all-important finger strength. Jumping right onto a difficult climb with cold fingers and arms generally results in a "flash pump." This is the phenomenon of an almost instantaneous swell and cramp that turns the forearms into useless chunks of pumped-out muscle. This can happen in a ridiculously short period of time, and can leave a climber unable to even tie shoelaces—for hours. Warm up your arms by gradually massaging your forearms and flexing wrists and fingers. Then start with very easy climbing. Gradually load your arms by climbing first on lower-angled terrain, then progressing to steeper and steeper walls. Also, start with large handholds and slowly move to smaller crimpers as you warm up. At the first hint of a pump, step off the wall and rest.

A good warm-up for most experienced climbers is simply to climb a couple of routes that are easy and straightforward. Repeating climbs that you have done several times before also helps because you know what to expect and will not be gripped by the fear of the unknown. The other sure way to get a flash pump is to start the gym session on a climb that is scary, because that leads to gripping way too tightly and climbing slowly. The warm-up period should last 10 to 15 minutes, or until you are feeling warm and loose, and all jitters have been worked out.

Traversing: One of the very best ways to warm up in a gym is by traversing. Traversing is climbing sideways across the wall. Most gyms allow climbers to traverse below a line that is 8 feet or so above the ground. That way the climber is never high off the deck, maybe a foot or so at the most, so ropes are not required. Traversing is a great activity for climbing in the gym by yourself. Good traversing technique has the climber moving with the hips parallel to the wall, shuffling hands and feet in one direction or the other. Try to stay on the inside edges of your feet. Try not to cross hands or feet. Imagine Spiderman moving sideways across the wall, hips in close to the wall and moving slowly and smoothly.

CLIMBING TRAINING

What is next, now that you are all good and warmed up? Go climbing! For most climbers, a session at the gym consists of moving about the gym, climbing different routes. Top-roping, leading, and bouldering—some will be easy, some hard, and you climb until you are too tired to hang on any longer. This in itself is great training. As the great rock climber and visionary Tony Yaniro once said, "Never pass up the opportunity to get pumped!" You will improve following this routine!

At some point, however, it is beneficial to apply some method to the rock-climbing training experience. Loosely borrowing from other sports, we can organize specific training for rock climbing around three concepts: endurance, strength or difficulty, and technique.

Endurance Training

Climbing endurance is the ability to hang on and climb for long periods of time. Endurance is not the same as strength. Strength equates with the ability to pull hard moves, such as long reaches, off small holds on an overhanging wall. Endurance is long-term muscle strength and is a great base from which to build strength. Endurance is developed by high repetition and low resistance (lots of easy climbing). In a rock gym, this means nonstop climbing generally using big handholds. Technical difficulty should be low and finger fatigue from crimping small holds should not be the limiting factor. The goal is the deep tissue all-out pump created by high-mileage climbing.

If you are alone and bouldering, then traversing about and linking walls together without resting on the ground is a great endurance exercise. Shoot for 30 minutes of continuous climbing. Practice good technique; hang straight on arms, use your feet, chalk up frequently, milk rest positions and stems. Climb up, down, left, and right and be creative about different routes and moves. Start with lower-angle walls and move onto overhanging terrain as endurance builds. Remember to try to use large handholds that naturally accommodate an open grip. Too much crimping on small holds leads to sore fingers, not pumped arms.

Think in terms of laps to practice endurance climbing on a top-rope or lead. Pick a difficulty level well within your limit. Remember that the goal is to climb continuously for several laps, so you do not want to be limited by technical difficulty. Try for five laps in a row. On a top-rope, for example, climb to the top, have your belayer lower you down, and without touching the ground, start back up again. Repeat until pumped.

Strength Training

One of the most gratifying aspects of climbing is the feeling of accomplishing harder climbs. This means that you are getting stronger, and it feels good. Strength is built by low repetitions and high resistance. In a climbing setting, then, this means attempting difficult climbs in a measured manner with long rests between burns. After a good warm-up, try climbs a little, or even way, above your comfort level. The goal is not usually to flash the route; redpointing is the more common objective. This refers to successfully climbing a route after previous attempts. Although redpointing generally refers to a style of lead climbing, the concept of working sections of a route and then linking them together also works well for top-roping or bouldering.

Difficult bouldering is also a great strength workout. A bouldering problem can be as short as a couple of moves, but success on those few moves can be both gratifying and beneficial in terms of strength gain. With each attempt at a move, not only is strength being used and built, but much subtle technique is also incorporated that is memorized into movement patterns for the next attempt. Linking a couple of hard moves requires concentration, power, and good technique.

Work a hard route on a rope by "hang-dogging." Although once used as a derogatory label, hangdogging is a legitimate technique for building strength. Climb till you fall, hang on the rope and rest, and try it again. Remember, the goal is not to hang on the rope, but to use the rope as a tool to allow you to build the strength and knowledge of a hard route so you can ultimately link all the moves together. Climbers refer to the routes that they are working on as "projects." Not everyone enjoys the project mentality; some climbers like to climb new things and do not like to fall. That is fine, too. But if you want to improve, you are probably going to fall.

Technique Training

There is no question that indoor climbing is the most effective medium for learning many basic climbing techniques. The modular holds and controlled environment found in a rock gym are ideal for simulating exact situations to train for and to memorize climbing positions and movement. The complexities of climbing technique can be broken down into some fundamental and universal moves that can be practiced with repetition and consistency indoors. Techniques for resting, weight transfer, body positioning, and movement are ideally suited for indoor training. There are, however, limitations to indoor climbing. The subtle nature of real rock is impossible to economically duplicate indoors, so many techniques such as crack climbing and friction climbing still require an outdoor apprentice-ship. Using the indoor walls with the intent of training for outdoor climbing can be very effective if some important differences between the two types of climbing are recognized.

One major difference between indoor and outdoor climbing is that indoor climbing terrain is generally easier to "read." In other words, the hand- and footholds indoors are obvious and easy to see; they protrude clearly from the wall. The top of the climb is clear. There is no mystery about where you are going and how much strength you need to conserve to get you there. Rarely while climbing indoors does one have to stop midroute and deal with equipment or protection problems. It is easy and common to climb indoors by literally taking a deep breath at the bottom of the wall and climbing in an all-out effort to reach the top.

Outdoor climbing is quite often the opposite. Hand- and footholds are difficult to see because they blend in with the rock. Sometimes it takes patience and poise to sort out the right holds. Outdoor routes can be long and devious. The climber must carefully pace his or her strength output. And outdoor climbing, especially multipitch traditional routes, requires that the climber is able to handle protection equipment and ropes with one hand, often while hanging from the other hand in the most precarious perches. All of these outdoor climbing demands mean that the climber must be in balance, relaxed, and efficient.

ROCK GYM TRAINING

Following are several technique drills and positions that can be practiced indoors with the intent of developing these types of outdoor climbing skills.

The Rest Position. This is a fundamental position for both indoor and outdoor climbing (defined in the Frequently Used Moves section earlier in this chapter). It is important to incorporate this position into a part of any indoor climbing workout. With one hand holding onto a good handhold, hang from that, straight arm. Keep your legs straight and relaxed. Ideally, your feet are on footholds at the same level as each other, so the body forms a stable tripod on the wall with three points of contact. The key to this position is keeping your hips pressed into the wall and your back slightly arched. To relax, drop the hand that is not on the hold and shake it out or chalk up. Train yourself to instinctively sag into a rest position every time you can while climbing in the gym. Not only does it help rest the nonholding arm (which is critical!), but it creates a habit that will be crucial to the outdoor transition. Remember that besides the need to rest and conserve strength, outdoor climbing demands many tasks, especially working with gear, to be performed with one hand. When you are climbing outdoors, assume the rest position when placing or removing protection. The rest position should become automatic whenever you reach a good handhold or jug.

Around the Clock. This is an excellent drill to learn basic weight transfer and balance. Locate four good holds—two handholds and two footholds—in a square configuration about shoulder-width apart, with the handholds at about eye level. The handholds should be comfortable to reach. With both hands and both feet on their respective holds, move your body around in a circle. Do not move your hands or feet, just your body. Move left, up, right, and down. Feel how shifting your weight to one side or the other changes your balance. Note that when you are in the upper position, your arm is "locked off," and in the lower position it is possible to assume a rest position off a straight arm.

This is a good way to warm up and stretch to begin a climbing session.

Variations to this exercise include *flagging*. Try flagging out by reaching up and right with the right hand while lifting the left foot off its foothold. The left foot works as a counterweight so that you can lean and reach farther with the right hand. In this position, only the left hand and the right foot have contact with the wall. Also try flagging in. Shift all your weight to the left foot and cross the right leg behind the left leg as a counterweight. This will balance you so that you can reach with the right hand to a hold up and over the left hand. The only two points of contact at this point are the left hand and the left foot.

Five Moving Parts. There are five parts that move when you climb: two hands, two feet, and one body. As you climb (preferably on an easy wall bristling with many good holds), concentrate on moving each part of your body separately and distinctly from the others. When reaching for a handhold, move nothing but that hand. The same goes for moving a foot. Try to freeze the rest of your body as you move a foot up to a hold. The key to these moves is in shifting your body weight as a separate move in a manner that keeps you in balance. This can be tricky. Learn to tune in to the subtle balance changes that occur as you shift your weight to one side or the other.

An example of the Five Moving Parts exercise is the following. Step up to a high foothold with the right foot. To accomplish this move, all of your weight is on the left foot. With the right foot established on the hold, shift the body weight to the right foot, rocking onto that hold. Now all weight is on the right foot, freeing the left foot to be moved up to a higher hold. This is the "crunch" position described in the Frequently Used Moves section earlier in this chapter. Both legs are now under you and in a position to raise you, primarily with the leg muscles. Now raise your body up and hold it in place by locking off one arm. The other arm now reaches high for the next hold, placing you in the rest position, ready to relax and analyze the moves that lie ahead.

The weight-shifting skills learned in this drill directly apply to outdoor climbing. Climbing in a gym creates a tendency to climb in a style wherein you move almost dynamically to the next hold. This is natural because you can so easily see the hold and determine whether it is good or not. Climbing this way, the climber flows toward the holds and is committed to reaching and sticking to the hold. Real rock is generally not so easy to read. You must be in balance as you feel about, searching for a potential hold. Remember that it is often prudent to test the quality of a real rock hold with a quick tap before committing to use it. Testing a hold is impossible unless you are in control of your movement. Good balance is especially critical while a climber is placing or removing protection. This exercise also illustrates how the legs can be incorporated more effectively during upward progression. The body is kept low, hanging on straight arms in the rest position as the legs are set underneath to powerfully raise the body. Learning how to propel yourself upward by pushing with the legs instead of pulling with the arms is a fundamental building-block of good technique.

Backstepping. This exercise is especially useful for sport climbers. When the angle of the climbing surface begins to overhang, it becomes more efficient to climb on the outside edges of the feet with the hips almost perpendicular to the wall. This is because it draws the center of gravity in closer to the wall, allowing more weight to be distributed to the feet, and encouraging a longer and more balanced reach. This is called "backstepping," and the best way to learn it is by drilling the movement repetitively on an overhanging, juggy route. Backstepping refers both to a way of specifically using a foothold and a way of moving upward.

Beginning with both hands on a starting hold, backstep—that is, place the outside edge of the left foot on a foothold ideally straight below the starting handholds. Shift weight onto the left foot and allow the right foot to swing forward (or flag) as a counterweight. Lock off with the right arm and reach up with the left hand to a hold. If this is done correctly, you will feel locked into place because of the balance generated by the backstep. To drill this move, continue climbing upward by rotating your body counterclockwise while hanging from the left arm until you can backstep with the right foot on an appropriate foothold. Do this rotation using as many intermediate footholds as necessary.

Now counterweight with the left leg and reach with the right arm to the next hold. Note that a good long reach should put you in a position to get a rest. Continue climbing in this manner, twisting back and forth, locking your hips into the wall and making long, balanced reaches to the next hold. This motion is a bit unnatural at first for many climbers, but repeated practice will make it second nature when you are at the crag.

Training With a Partner

If you have a training partner at the gym, the possibilities for interesting training are limited only by your imagination. Strength, endurance, and balance can all be improved by training with your partner. Here are a few ideas:

- Pick a route well within your abilities and do laps, each time eliminating a key hold.
- Climb blindfolded, with your belayer giving verbal directions to each hold—this is really good for developing balance and learning body positioning.
- Do "Simon Says" traverses, with your partner pointing out each hold—you will find yourself in some bizarre positions but do not worry, you can get even when it is your partner's turn to traverse!
- Have a competition to get "no hands" rests—you will be amazed at where you can drop your hands when you practice.
- Have a dynamic move competition—warm up, do not use crimpers, and be careful not to risk injury while you build confidence.
- Climb easy routes one-handed, with your partner calling out the handholds.
- Climb a route using just side pulls, underclings, et cetera, with your partner calling out the handholds.
- Climb a route making every move a high-step, or never using a handhold above your shoulder, et cetera, then have your partner try the route using the same hold sequence.

You get the idea; have fun, try new things, make the gym a fun place to train!

Indoor Moves

To help make the transition to the outdoors smoother, it helps to use the indoor environment to practice some of the skills that will be needed outside.

Jamming. If the wall has any cracks—even if they are not very good simulations of outdoor cracks—practice jamming on them. Indoor cracks usually are not the most popular routes in the gym, which means there probably will not be a line! To make the most of any crack try:

- making as many jams as possible
- making as few jams as possible
- making every foothold a jam (this is hard to do when good footholds abound on either side!)
- downclimbing the crack
- liebacking all the way up and down

Smearing. Another skill that is rarely perfected indoors is smearing—pasting your feet on the wall when there is no obvious hold. Most indoor walls are so littered with holds that footholds are automatic. Try your favorite route without using any of the bolted holds. You may be surprised at how many tiny features on the surface of the wall make good smears.

Stemming. Inside corners offer great opportunities to improve your stemming.

FINGERBOARD TRAINING

Fingerboards are also very effective tools for developing climbing-specific upper-body strength, especially the contact strength of fingers and forearms. They are constructed of molded resin or wood and have handholds of various sizes. Mounted above a doorway or set away from a wall, a fingerboard is one of the best training tools other than a climbing wall. Fingerboards are not for novices; a base of strength built by a season of easy climbing and bouldering is recommended before launching into a fingerboard training session. Always warm up thoroughly before beginning a fingerboard session.

A couple of tips for proper use of fingerboards: Many of the exercises involve static hangs off certain handholds. When performing a hang, keep the elbows and shoulders slightly flexed so that the body is supported by the muscles in the arms. Do not hang in a dead hang with your weight supported by fully extended shoulders and elbows. A dead hang is very stressful on the joints and connections in the shoulders and elbows.

Try not to crimp on small holds. A crimp hold hyperextends the joints of the fingers. Crimping provides a superstrong lock onto a small hold, but repetitive use of this type of hold in a training environment can overtax the joints and lead to sore, swollen, and stiff fingers. Use an open grip instead. This is not an easy hold to master, especially on smaller holds. The best way to build open grip strength is on sloping handholds. Start with large slopers, gradually moving onto smaller and smaller holds over the course of a training season.

Note that at this level, proper training technique differs from good climbing technique. For example, the rest position used while climbing has the climber relaxing all the body weight on a straight arm. This position rests the arm muscles by relying on the bones and skeletal system to bear the brunt of the body weight. Using that position for repetitive and lengthy fingerboard training could potentially lead to injury. Remember that training is not climbing. The point of training is to efficiently and safely exhaust and rebuild climbing-specific strength.

As with training on a climbing wall, fingerboard training can be broken into the two categories of endurance and strength training. Endurance exercises on a fingerboard consist typically of longer timed hangs on larger holds. For example, start by timing yourself for your maximum hang time on the largest holds on the board. Rest a couple of minutes, and repeat your maximum hang. See how many times you can repeat this cycle of maximum hangs and rests. Move to sloping holds or smaller edges (but do not crimp!) to increase the challenge. Try the "20/20" exercise: hang for 20 seconds, then rest for 20 seconds. Repeat ten times.

Power workouts demand maximum effort for a short duration. Longer rests between sets may be necessary. Time yourself for maximum hang time on progressively smaller holds. If hang time exceeds 10 seconds, then move to a smaller hold. Include pull-ups in a fingerboard routine. To build strength on a fingerboard, the size of the hold should only allow five pull-ups at most. If you can do more, move to smaller holds. More strength can be developed by adding resistance. Hang weights in 2-pound increments from your chalk-bag belt and repeat your usual routine. It will be a lot harder, and is an excellent illustration of the importance of climbing with as little weight on your body as possible!

CHAPTER 2

Sport Climbing Outdoors

Do you feel the rush of fresh air? We have just opened the door to the gym and are about to step outside. This is a wonderful moment. For many, climbing outdoors is what rock climbing is all about. But it also is a potentially dangerous step. If you walk out the climbing gym door unprepared to meet the technical challenges and face the hazards, you take unnecessary risks. This chapter will help prepare you to meet those challenges and move outdoors as safely as possible. This chapter focuses on the techniques for safely top-roping and leading single-pitch rock climbs, working through the following progression:

- belaying outdoors
- top-roping on fixed anchors
- leading single-pitch climbs with fixed protection and anchors

So what is so different about being outside? Almost everything. And that is the challenge. Climbers see the same equipment and the same moves, hear the same banter, and assume that climbing outside is just like climbing in a gym with the roof off. But you cannot get hit by lightning at the local rock

gym. Or get caught in the dark. Or rappel off the end of your rope. Climbers indoors can be casual about some things; climbers outside must be cautious about everything. Here are a few examples to drive the point home:

- In the gym the bolts, anchors, and quickdraws are in place and their condition is monitored by the gym staff; outdoors there may not be bolts or anchors and almost certainly no quickdraws, and no one is responsible for inspecting anything.
- In the gym you rarely have to worry about your safety on the approach or descent from a climb—stumble and you might get a rug burn; outside you can be struck by a rock while you are standing at the base of a route or fall off a cliff while setting up a top-rope.
- Indoors you do not have to worry about sunburn, rockfall, dangerous trails, poisonous animals or plants, rain, lightning, heat, cold, loose rock, or dead batteries in your cell phone; outside, you better be prepared to deal with all these things and more.

Climbers often get in trouble because they make bad decisions. Most often these bad decisions are the result of being unskilled, unaware, or brazen. Learn the skills, stay alert, err on the side of caution, and you will maximize your safety. Then you can concentrate on having fun!

PRETRIP PLANNING

A lot of the hazards in climbing outside can be minimized (and the enjoyment maximized) by doing your homework before you head out the door.

- Get a guidebook to the area you intend to climb—and read it.
- Find out if there are any hazards to prepare for: rough approaches or descents, loose rock, difficult places to set anchors (in other words, it may be hard or dangerous to get to the top of the route to set the top anchor).
- Be certain that you have all the proper equipment, including adequate clothing, food, and water.
- Make sure that the type of climbing and the difficulty levels suit your experience level.

- Be certain that you are technically prepared to handle the safety system requirements (for example, if you go to a sport-climbing area where all the routes are longer than half a pitch, you better know how to tie two ropes together, belay with a knot in the system, thread an anchor, and rappel off).

HAZARD ASSESSMENT AND SAFETY MANAGEMENT

Everyone knows climbing is dangerous—that is why every book like this one has a disclaimer. So what are the risks and how can they be minimized? Risks fall into two categories: objective and subjective.

Objective hazards are those inherent in climbing outdoors and are often environment-related: rockfall, weather, the difficulty and dangers of approaches and descents. Objective hazards can be assessed and often reduced by the climber—if the rock is very loose, climb elsewhere; if the weather is threatening, leave early. Accidents arising from objective hazards are often deemed "acts of God."

Subjective hazards are those brought to the crags by the climbers themselves: poor route choices, bad anchors, being sloppy or casual, not taking reasonable precautions, cutting corners. Subjective hazards can be controlled by the climber knowing his or her limits, staying alert, and being technically prepared for emergencies. Accidents arising from subjective hazards are usually blamed on "pilot error."

In order to minimize risk, climbers must recognize and assess the various hazards and create safety management systems to deal with them. Hazards can be as big as a thunderhead or as small as a loose bolt hanger. Safe climbing requires that hazards be continuously analyzed and managed on both the macro and micro level. Climbers need to be aware of the weather and at the same time be diligent about buckling their harness and tying their knots correctly; they must recognize the rockfall potential, and put their helmet on. Building a great anchor but failing to keep an eye on the western sky can put you at significant risk.

APPROACHES AND DESCENTS

Sometimes getting to the climb and returning to the car can be more dangerous than climbing the route itself—at least you are belayed while climbing. An alarming number of accidents occur just getting to and from the climb: climbers slip on wet slabs, stumble on teetering talus blocks, trip on tree roots, fall off short cliffs, and wade through poison ivy—all the time with their eyes dreamily focused on the crags. Do not forget to look at your feet on the way in, and do not let your guard down on the way back to the car. One of the authors once fell off a 200-foot cliff walking down after finishing a route—he landed on the only ledge and was fortunate to walk away with just a bad limp and an education.

EDGES AND TRICKY TERRAIN

A dangerous edge is any precipice you can fall off, or that can drop something on you. It does not take much of an edge for it to be dangerous. While the top or bottom of a big cliff is obviously dangerous, people often fail to realize that a short slab or section of talus also can be hazardous. Be a prudent climber, stay alert on even the most benign terrain, and be quick to take precautions: Detour around the slab, pick a better line through the talus, put your helmet on before reaching the cliff (you have to carry it anyway, so you might as well carry it on your head).

When you get to the cliff, look for hazards: loose rock, climbers above, irregular ground at the base that could make belaying difficult, poison ivy, et cetera. If hazards exist, do your best to avoid them: Choose the most solid route and position people on the ground out of the fall line, climb to the side of other parties, pick the best spot for the belayer and position him or her to maximize stability.

FALLING OBJECTS

Okay, so you made it safely to the crag, assessing hazards and making the right decisions along the way. The harnesses, shoes, and helmets are on and the climber is about to make the crux moves. Everything is under control, when suddenly you hear a cry from above: "*Rock!*" This is the universal cry that indicates something is falling. It alerts all other climbers of a potential hazard. If you see something fall, yell "*Rock*" loudly and keep yelling until the object is on the ground—and yell it even if you think you are alone in the area. What should you do if you hear someone yell "*Rock*"? Get very small under your helmet, do not panic, and:

- Stay put. Running away could be dangerous and is rarely the best action; after all, "over there" is not necessarily any better than where you are; the only exception would be if you can quickly get under cover without putting anyone else in danger (running while belaying can be dangerous to the climber).
- Do not look up. It sounds obvious, but it is not; train yourself to keep a level head (one exception might be when the alarm comes from very high above or way off to the side—in these instances, a quick look may help you determine whether you need to do something to avoid getting hit).
- Do not look down. If you are going to get hit in the head, it should be the top of your helmet, not your neck, that takes the impact.
- Keep your arms at your sides. Be a small target—and do not put your hands on top of your head; your helmet will protect your head better than your hands can.

CLIMBING ETIQUETTE

ENVIRONMENTAL CONCERNS

Climbers are one of the most environmentally friendly user-groups. They are usually conscientious, follow the rules, and pack out their trash. Help keep up the good reputation by following the general principles established by Leave No Trace, a national nonprofit organization committed to minimizing environmental impacts by recreationalists:

- Plan ahead and prepare.
- Camp and travel on durable surfaces.
- Pack it in, pack it out.
- Properly dispose of what you cannot pack out.
- Leave what you find.
- Minimize use and impact from fires.

  In addition, follow these specific principles when rock climbing:
- Do not chip or drill holds.
- Use removable protection. Bolts and pitons permanently change the rock.
- Do not use motorized drills in wilderness areas. Placing bolts is a privilege; follow the rules.
- Consider the overall environmental impacts of developing a new area or route. Traffic, trails, and disturbance to wildlife may follow.
- Leave anchors that blend in with the rock. If you place bolts on a route, leave a fixed anchor at the belay, or leave a sling, and make them as invisible as possible.
- Do not rappel directly from trees. Use dull-colored slings and rappel rings instead; trees can die if they are rappelled from repeatedly.
- Consider choosing a chalk color that blends in with the rock—or using none at all.
- Clean up after yourself. Spend a few minutes cleaning up before you leave.
- Keep the noise down, especially in urban areas. Be sensitive to the solitude enjoyed by residents and other users.
- Park where you should, and keep a low profile along the road too.
- Ask permission—private land is often open to climbers; help keep it that way by checking with the land owners if you have any doubt about access privileges. Follow regulations, respect closures (for example, for nesting raptors), get involved to solve access problems, consider joining the Access Fund (303-545-6772), a climber advocacy group that works to keep climbing areas open to climbers.

ETHICS

College degrees are offered in this subject, but here we do not need to get that deep. For climbers it is common sense to:

- Be kind to climbers, land owners, and other users. Be sensitive, not a nuisance.
- Do not hog routes.
- Do not pressure other climbers to hurry up with your favorite climb; do something else while you wait.
- Do not mislead other climbers about the characteristics of a route. "Sandbagging" can be dangerous.
- Be cautious about sharing routes. Be certain of the safety system's security before climbing on any rope (one of the authors once had a close call when a climber offered to let him use his top-rope—the climber had threaded the rope directly through a sling instead of through carabiners).
- Be quick to help in an emergency. Keep your eyes open, step in if you see a life-threatening situation developing, help if you can if there is an accident, let the person with the most medical experience take charge.

EQUIPMENT

Climbing routes outdoors with fixed anchors require only a few more pieces of equipment in addition to what you use indoors. The most obvious is a helmet. Though this essential piece of equipment is covered in chapter 1, Indoor Climbing—The Fundamentals, it is used primarily outdoors rather than in rock gyms. Always consider using one outdoors. A few other things to bring with you into the great outdoors include:

- The Ten Essentials: extra clothing and extra food (both covered in chapter 1, Indoor Climbing—The Fundamentals), plus a

CHART 1

	Indoors	Outdoors
Belay Terrain	flat	flat, sloping, or hanging
	smooth	smooth or uneven
	solid	solid or unstable
	safe	safe or dangerous
Access to Belay Anchor	always safe, a walk across the floor	can be safe, can be dangerous, may require a belay
Belayer Position	always below the climber	below or above the climber
Belay Device	all will work equally well, no judgment is required	all will work, but safety is dependent on the system chosen, and judgment is required
Belay Technique	always off harness	off harness, off anchor, off remote anchor, redirected, or off extended anchor

headlamp, a compass, a map, a knife, a lighter or matches in a waterproof container, firestarter, sunglasses or other UV eye protection, and a first-aid kit—they do not weigh much and could prove valuable if you head into the backcountry
- Sunscreen, insect repellent, jacket, hat, gloves—remember, we are not in a climate-controlled environment anymore
- Cell phone—high-tech encumbrance or prudent piece of safety equipment? Your choice.

BELAYING OUTDOORS

Belaying is belaying, right? Well, not really. Belaying indoors is always the same: You stand on the floor and belay either a lead or a toprope. Belaying outdoors is not so simple. You may be positioned below the climber, maybe above; the ground may be flat, sloping, or rocky, or you may be hanging off the belay; you may or may not need to be anchored; reaching the belay anchor may be as straightforward as walking up to the base of the route (as in a gym) or require a rappel or a belay from above. Belaying outdoors involves making decisions about the anchor, the position of the belayer, and the belay technique. Being able to safely set up belays in a wide range of outdoor situations requires an understanding of the system options, the technical proficiency to set up correctly the chosen system, and the maturity to know your limits. Learn the systems, pick the best option for the situation, but do not experiment—if you move out of your comfort zone, you may put yourself and others at risk.

There is common ground between belaying indoors and outdoors. The actions of belaying (paying rope out, taking rope in, catching falls, lowering climbers) and the tools (plates, tubes, auto-locking devices, and the Munter hitch) are all the same. The difference is in the application of the actions and the tools.

You can see in Chart 1 that many more variables exist outside, and a lot more decisions must be made. Analyze each climb. Learn the techniques. Choose the safest options.

The CATCH principles: It is imperative when climbing outdoors that the belayer is prepared to catch a fall. Unlike in the perfect environment of the gym, climbing outdoors has too many variables to allow for casual belaying. To help ensure safety, adhere to the following **CATCH** principles:

C—Be sure the system is *closed* by having the belayer tie into the rope.

A—*Align* the belayer between the anchor and the anticipated direction of force.

T—Have the belayer positioned *tight* to the belay anchor.

C—Be sure the *communication* is clear between the climber and the belayer.

H—Be sure the belayer's brake *hand* is on the rope and he or she can belay safely.

Closed. Closing the system is fundamental in climbing—we do it when we back-buckle our harness and tie a keeper knot in our figure eight knot—and is very important in belaying. Climbers are injured each year when their belayer drops them because the end of the rope passes completely through the belay device. The simplest way to close the system is just to have the belayer tie the end of his or her rope to the harness—the belayer has to tie in to climb the route anyway. If the belayer is not planning to climb the route, then he or she can close the system by tying a figure eight on a bight below the belay device.

*This belayer has followed the **CATCH** principles and is ready to catch a falling climber.*

Aligned. Whenever possible the belayer should be clipped into an anchor on the ground, either with the climbing rope or with slings girth-hitched to the harness. After clipping in, the belayer should determine the most likely direction he or she will be pulled if the leader falls, and align with it. A falling leader will create a straight line between the first piece of protection and the anchor, and the belayer, if not aligned with that, can be pulled out of position.

Tight. Just being in line between the anchor

KEY TRANSITION EXERCISE:
LEARNING THE VITAL SKILLS FOR CLIMBING OUTSIDE
How to Belay from an Anchor Correctly, Using the CATCH Principles

The Challenge

Belaying properly is one of the most vital skills a climber will ever master. This exercise is designed to help the climber quickly master the fundamental principles.

The Difference Between Belaying Indoors and Belaying Outdoors

Indoors: Belaying indoors is consistent and simple: The belayer stands on the floor and belays a lead top-rope off the harness. The belayer may or may not be tied in. Catching a fall is always a matter of locking off the device and leaning back.

Outdoors: Belaying outdoors is variable and often complicated; no two belay setups are precisely the same. Belayers always need to be ready and able to **CATCH** a fall.

The Goal

Master basic belaying by learning the five key safety principles.

The Equipment

2 climbing harnesses
2 locking carabiners
1 two-point anchor
1 rope
1 belay/rappel device

The Setup

The standard two-point anchor setup or, even easier, a single-point anchor consisting of a sling girth-hitched around a tree or post, can be used (see the How to Use This Book section of the Introduction).

The CATCH Exercise

Here is a quick review of the **CATCH** principles:

C—*Close* the system by having both the climber and the belayer tie in to the rope.

A—*Align* the belayer between the anchor and the anticipated direction of force.

T—Keep the belayer *tight* to the anchor.

C—Be certain that the *communication* between the climber and the belayer is clear.

H—Make sure the belayer's brake *hand* is on the rope and he or she can belay properly.

1. Both the climber and belayer tie into the rope—this closes the system.
2. The belayer ties a figure eight on a bight loop, and clips it to the master point of the anchor with a locking carabiner to create the tie-in.
3. The belayer aligns him or herself between the anchor and the direction the climber is going to pull from.
4. The belayer leans off the anchor, making him or herself tight to the anchor (adjust the length of the tie-in if necessary).
5. The belayer puts the climber on belay with a tube or plate device on the harness and prepares to belay.
6. Using the proper signals ("on belay," "climbing," et cetera), the belayer feeds rope out of the system while the climber slowly walks away from him or her 15 or 20 feet.
7. The climber now walks toward the belay while the belayer practices taking in rope without letting go of the brake hand; the climber can load the system occasionally by leaning back to simulate catching an easy fall.
8. Repeat steps 6 and 7, each time violating a principle: Have the belayer try to catch a fall when out of alignment with the anchor or with slack between them and the anchor, or have the climber weight the system when the belayer's brake hand is off the rope—the resulting loss of control will drive home the need to always be ready to **CATCH** a fall.
9. Switch positions and repeat the exercise.

and the anticipated direction of force is not enough. The belayer must also be positioned tight to the belay anchor; if not, he or she risks being pulled until positioned tight and could lose control.

Communication. Before leaving the ground, the climber must communicate clearly with the belayer about what is going to happen. Will the leader be lowered after clipping the top anchors? Will the leader rappel? In the first situation, the belayer must keep the leader on belay; in the second, the belayer will take the leader off belay while he or she rigs the rappel. If the leader expects to be lowered and the belayer expects him or her to rappel, there could be fatal consequences. Get your communication clear.

Hand. It seems like such a simple thing: Feed rope in and take rope out without letting go of

the brake hand. It is amazing how frequently climbers—especially novices—fail to do this correctly. Before the climber leaves the ground, be absolutely sure that the belayer can and will keep the belay in effect until the climb is over. An extra 10 minutes on the ground practicing could save the climber's life.

TOP-ROPING ON FIXED ANCHORS

Top-roping outside on fixed anchors is most like climbing in the gym, and is the logical first step outdoors. At sport-climbing areas, the typical top-rope belay setup is identical to that so well known indoors: the slingshot belay. Two other situations that this section addresses are how to rig a slingshot top-rope on routes that are longer than half a rope length, and how to safely top-rope mildly overhanging or traversing routes.

THE SLINGSHOT BELAY

In the slingshot belay, whether indoors or outdoors, the rope runs from the belayer up through the top anchor and back down to the climber. There is one very important difference outdoors, however: The rope is not fixed in place; it must be put through the anchor by the climbers themselves. How safely this can be accomplished for a given climb depends on the terrain and the skill and judgment of the climbers. A short cliff with a flat, easily accessible top and bolts just below the edge is a simple and relatively safe place to set up a top-rope. But climbing areas this straightforward are not typical. At many crags, the top may be uneven or sloping, requiring a belay just to get to the anchors. Another cliff may not have access to the top belay at all and will require that routes be led before a top-rope can be established (for example, short routes at the base of tall cliffs). And still another cliff may not have fixed anchors at all and the climbers will have to build their own (see chapter 3, Traditional (Rock) Climbing).

The characteristics of a cliff are usually clearly described in a guidebook. Read the description prior to heading out to make sure that you will be able to set up your climbs safely. If you do not feel technically capable of arranging the belays safely, go somewhere else that day. Then practice the necessary techniques on the ground before your next trip. Assuming that the area where you intend to go is ideal, what decisions need to be made?

1. Consult the guidebook and choose a route within your abilities. Outdoor routes do not have the name and grade labeled at the base or have the holds conveniently marked with colored tape.

2. Determine how you are going to approach the anchor safely. It may be reasonably safe to walk to the top, reach over, and clip the anchor, but do not hesitate to belay the operation from above if there is any chance of slipping.

3. Be certain that you have clipped the anchor as safely as possible. Assuming a standard two-bolt anchor, the options are as follows: (a) clip an oval or D carabiner to each bolt, then clip a 24-inch-long $9/16$-inch or larger sling into both bolts, and clip a pair of reversed and opposed carabiners (locking preferred) into the sling using the "magic X" technique—and keep in mind that if the sling fails, the system fails; or (b) clip a quickdraw to each bolt so that the two lower carabiners are oriented reversed and opposed, then clip the rope in at its center point. These two techniques establish the "master point" of the anchor—the point where everything comes together. Do not thread the rope through the anchor bolts, even if they are designed for lowering or if a chain and ring are available; it can be hard to pull the rope and causes unnecessary wear. If the master point created is higher than the lowering ring on the fixed anchor, then you can run the rope through the fixed anchor to back up the slings. This will also preposition the rope for lowering or rappelling later.

4. After the anchor is clipped, the rope threaded, and the carabiners properly aligned and locked, confirm that both rope ends reach the ground and then

Don't ever hesitate to give a belay while setting up an anchor at the edge of a cliff.

have someone on the ground test-pull the rope to make sure it runs smoothly.

5. When you get back down to the base of the route, determine whether the belayer should be anchored—you might decide this is a good idea if the belayer is much lighter than the climber; the terrain at the bottom is uneven, unstable, sloping, or on a ledge; or the belayer cannot belay from directly below the climb.

6. Decide what happens when the climber reaches the anchor: lower off immediately, clip in, clean the anchor, and then lower off; or clip in, clean the anchor, and rappel off. It is critical for the belayer and climber to agree about this. An unfortunate number of accidents occur when the belayer and climber fail to communicate clearly.

You can see by these six points that just the simple act of setting up a slingshot belay at a straightforward location outdoors requires far more thought and judgment than

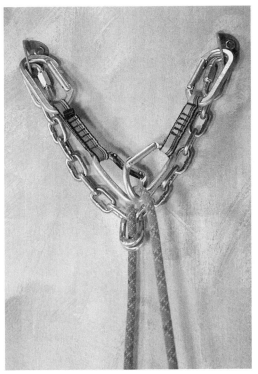

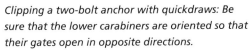

Clipping a two-bolt anchor with quickdraws: Be sure that the lower carabiners are oriented so that their gates open in opposite directions.

If the permanent lowering ring on the anchor is lower than the bottom carabiners on your quickdraws then you can thread it when you create the anchor. It will back up the quickdraws and make it easier to clean if the last person is going to lower off—all he has to do is remove the quickdraws.

using the identical setup indoors. And it is not over yet.

What do you do when the last climber is finished? How do you remove the anchor? In the simplest situations, the best thing to do is lower the last climber down, then walk back up to the top and safely take the anchor apart.

If that option is difficult or dangerous for any reason, the last climber up can clean the anchor and either be lowered or rappel from the anchor bolts. To be done safely, both techniques require clear communication between climber and belayer, and a specific series of steps must be performed.

KEY TRANSITION EXERCISE: LEARNING THE VITAL SKILLS FOR CLIMBING OUTSIDE
How to Clean a Top-Rope and Be Lowered Down or Rappel Down

THE CHALLENGE

Many anchors consist of two bolts and either chains or slings with a fixed ring; the climber creates the belay anchor by clipping in to the bolts with a pair of quickdraws. If the quickdraws cannot be removed safely or conveniently from above, how do you get them back? Typically, the last climber cleans the quickdraws from the bolts, threads the rope through the fixed anchor, and then is either lowered by the belayer or rappels down the route.

However, this transition is complicated and can be very risky if not done properly. An alarming number of accidents are the result of making mistakes during this transition. Performing the following exercise near the ground will help develop competence and confidence in the system so that the real transition 80 feet up in the air can be accomplished safely.

Descending from fixed anchor bolts by lowering or rappelling is only possible when the bolt hangers are designed for lowering, or when a chain and lowering ring or webbing and rappel rings are in place. Never perform a lower or rappel through webbing alone—it can easily be melted and fail—or from standard bolt hangers, which can damage the rope.

THE DIFFERENCE BETWEEN CLEANING A TOP-ROPE INDOORS AND OUTDOORS

Indoors: You do not clean a top-rope inside. They are prerigged. You climb the route, lean back on the rope, and are lowered back down by your belayer.
Outdoors: Top-ropes are not prerigged outside. You must rig the top-rope yourself, climb the route, and then dismantle the anchor and descend without compromising safety.

THE GOAL

Master the techniques for cleaning a top-rope and descending by being lowered or by rappelling.

THE EQUIPMENT

    2 climbing harnesses
    4 24-inch slings
    4 locking carabiners
    2 belay/rappel devices
    1 rope
    7 nonlocking carabiners
    2 quickdraws
    1 two-point anchor

THE SETUP

The standard two-point anchor setup is all you need (see How to Use This Book in the Introduction).

The Lowering Exercise

The following steps assume that the fixed anchor has not been prethreaded. If the fixed anchor was built so that the lowering ring at the bottom is lower than the bottom carabiners on the quickdraws, the lowering ring can be threaded in addition to the quickdraws to rig the top-rope. The climber's weight will be held by the quickdraws, and when the last climber reaches the anchor, all he or she needs to do is take his or her weight off the rope momentarily and unclip the quickdraws. Since his or her rope is already through the fixed lowering ring, all the last climber needs to do is sit back and be lowered down by the belayer. If the anchor cannot be rigged this way, or if the route is led first, then take the following steps to clean the quickdraws and descend:

1. Clip a quickdraw to each anchor point so that the gates on the lower carabiners are opposed.
2. Put the rope through the lower carabiner of each quickdraw—but not through the fixed anchor.

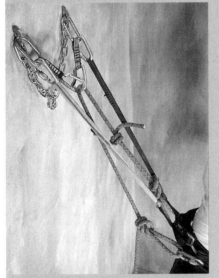

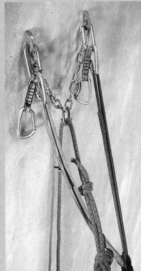

The climber clips into the anchor with slings girth-hitched to his harness, ties an overhand on a bight knot on the rope and clips it to his harness.

The climber unties the rope from his harness, threads it through the permanent lowering ring on the anchor, and then ties back in.

The climber pulls up to the anchor, has the belayer hold him there, removes the slings and quickdraws, and then the belayer lowers the climber to the ground.

3. The climber and the belayer tie in to each end of the rope.
4. The belayer takes the slack out of the system and puts the climber on belay.
5. The climber girth-hitches the two 24-inch slings to his or her harness and then clips each sling to the gear loops on the harness—one on the left side and one on the right side.
6. The climber pulls up to the quickdraws; the belayer locks off the rope and holds the climber.
7. The climber clips the slings that are girth-hitched to his or her harness to each anchor point.
8. The belayer lowers the climber onto the slings and then feeds out 6 to 8 feet of slack.
9. The climber pulls up the slack, ties an overhand on a bight, and clips it to a gear loop on the harness with a nonlocking carabiner; this ensures that the rope will not be dropped during the transition.
10. The climber unties the rope from the harness, threads the end through the fixed master point—the lap link—and then ties back in to the harness.
11. The climber unties the overhand knot, pulls up to the anchor, and has the belayer lock off the rope—all the climber's weight should now be on the lap link.
12. The climber unclips the quickdraws and the two slings girth-hitched to the harness.
13. The belayer lowers the climber down.
14. Repeat steps 4 through 13, with the belayer and climber switching positions—and keep practicing until both people feel completely comfortable with the steps.

The Rappelling Exercise—With an Autoblock Backup

This exercise is for those occasions when the last climber chooses to rappel instead of being lowered.

1. Have the climber carry two 24-inch slings over the shoulder, and have one rappel device and two locking carabiners clipped to a gear loop on the harness.
2. Repeat steps 1 through 9 as in the lowering exercise above—the belayer is no longer necessary.
3. The climber unties the rope from his or her harness, threads the end through the fixed master point, ties a second overhand on a bight, and clips it to his or her harness.
4. The climber unties the first overhand backup and pulls enough rope through the fixed anchor so that both ends will be on the ground (on most routes, this will be about half the length of the rope; for this exercise, far less is needed).
5. The climber unties the second backup overhand knot and drops the rope.
6. The climber doubles one of the two remaining 24-inch slings through the harness and clips the locking carabiner with the rappel device to it (follow manufacturer's instructions on where to tie in to the harness for a rappel—many harnesses come with a sewn loop exactly for this purpose).
7. The climber pulls up slack on the double rappel rope, threads the rappel device, clips it in, and locks the carabiner.
8. The climber attaches the remaining locking carabiner to the harness and clips the remaining 24-inch sling to it.

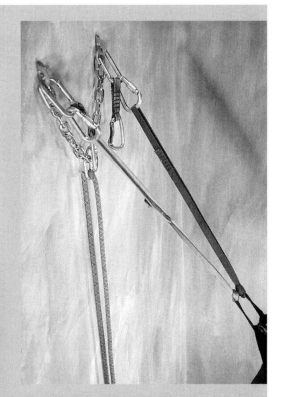

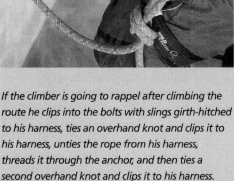

If the climber is going to rappel after climbing the route he clips into the bolts with slings girth-hitched to his harness, ties an overhand knot and clips it to his harness, unties the rope from his harness, threads it through the anchor, and then ties a second overhand knot and clips it to his harness.

The climber unties the overhand knot on the standing end of the rope (the end that leads to the ground) and then pulls half the rope through the anchor (the second overhand knot ensures that the rope cannot be dropped during the operation).

9. The climber clips the second locking carabiner to the harness, clips in the second sling to it, then wraps the sling around the double rappel rope four to six times just below the rappel device (the more wraps, the greater the friction), clips the sling back into the carabiner, and locks it. This creates the autoblock backup.

10. The climber pulls up tight to the anchor, takes all the slack out between the rappel device and the anchor, and weights the rappel, engaging the autoblock; all the climber's weight should now be on the rope, and the original anchor slings should be loose.

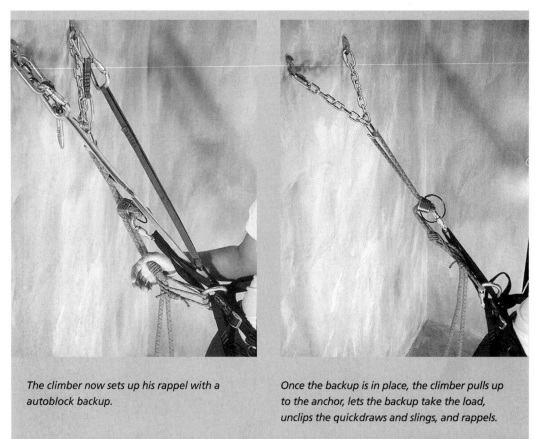

The climber now sets up his rappel with a autoblock backup.

Once the backup is in place, the climber pulls up to the anchor, lets the backup take the load, unclips the quickdraws and slings, and rappels.

11. The climber removes the original girth-hitched slings and stores them by clipping them back to the gear loops.
12. The climber removes the original quickdraws and rappels using the autoblock as a backup.
13. Repeat steps 1 through 12, with the climbers switching positions.

ON ROUTES LONGER THAN HALF A ROPE LENGTH

On routes that are longer than half a rope length (when a 165-foot rope is not long enough to set up a slingshot belay), how do you rig a slingshot top-rope? The simplest option may be to belay from above, allowing the climber to be belayed safely with one rope. Belaying from above is described in chapter 3, Traditional (Rock) Climbing. However, the climb can still be belayed using the slingshot system if two ropes are tied together. This will present a problem, though, if the climb is less than 165 feet long. If the route is 100 feet long and the climber ties in to one end of the rope, the rope will run from the climber, up through the anchor, back down

65 feet to the knot, and then another 35 feet to the belayer. When the climber gets 35 feet off the ground, the knot will reach the belayer and he or she will have to make a technical and potentially dangerous knot pass. The belayer will also have to repeat the knot pass when lowering the climber down after the ascent.

But do not panic; there is a wonderfully simple solution. The climber ties in at the point where the rope reaches the ground, instead of at the end of the rope. The climber will trail 65 feet of rope behind him or her (no big deal, just like leading), will reach the anchor at the same time that the knot reaches the belayer, and can be easily lowered back down—no knot pass is necessary. The trick is how to tie in. Bulky knots such as a retraced figure eight can be used, as well as opposed and reversed carabiners, but a simpler solution is this:

1. Position the knot on the belayer's side of the top anchor.
2. At the point where the climber's side of the rope reaches the ground, tie a figure eight on a bight, creating at least a 3-foot loop.

 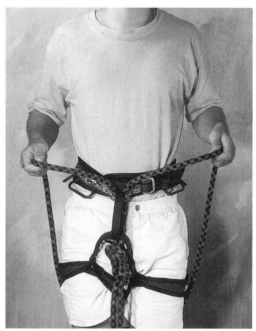

Tying into the middle of the rope to top-rope routes longer than half a rope length.

Step one: Tie a figure eight on a bight with a big loop (at least 3 feet).
Step two: Pass the loop through the tie-in point of the harness until the figure eight knot reaches it.

Step two continued: Pass the loop over your head and begin to work it down to your feet.

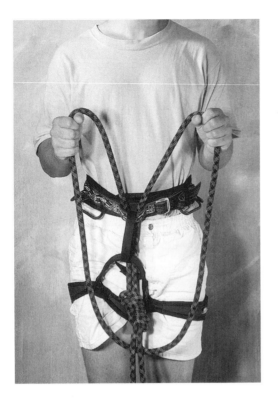

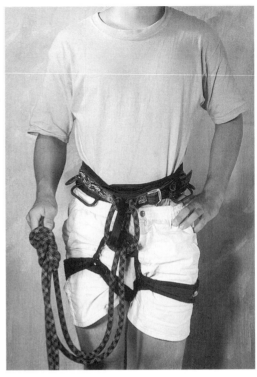

Step three: Step through the loop and bring it up in front of you.

Step four: Cinch the loop around the harness loosely.

3. Pass the loop through the harness, over the climber's head, down around his or her feet, and back up to the harness again—creating a girth hitch directly on the harness.

4. Feed all the slack through the figure eight and tighten up the girth hitch to create a snug, secure connection.

5. To help the trailed section of rope stay out of the climber's way, tie an overhand loop about 18 feet down the free end and clip it to the back of the climber's harness—this keeps the free end hanging behind the climber and out of the way of his or her feet.

This may sound complicated, but it is not. It is a quick, straightforward, and very secure midrope tie-in with little bulk.

ON OVERHANGING OR TRAVERSING ROUTES

Setting up a top-rope on an overhanging or traversing route may require special preparations before the route can be safely climbed.

Step five: Feed all the slack through the figure eight knot and tighten the girth hitch around the harness until snug.

If the route is only gently overhanging or the traversing is minimal, the basic slingshot setup may be suitable. But on more steeply overhanging routes or when the climb traverses more than a few feet, the basic setup will probably not be safe enough. A climber falling on these routes will swing, and this could cause him or her to strike the ground, trees, or other features on the cliff, or it may simply put the climber so far off route that he or she cannot resume climbing.

Routes in which this swinging hazard exists must be equipped differently. To minimize the swing potential, the climbing rope must run through some or all of the climb's protection bolts. This requires that the climber setting up the top anchor be lowered down the route and held in close to the rock by the belayer so he or she can clip the bolts. Assuming that the anchor can be established easily and safely from above, here are the steps to equip the route:

1. The climber at the anchor clips the top anchor, establishes the master point, puts the rope through it, and ties in.
2. Meanwhile, the belayer clips the climbing rope through a quickdraw on the first protection bolt; this will help the climber stay as close to the route as possible during the lowering (if the bolt cannot be reached safely by bouldering up a move or two, consider climbing a different route).
3. The belayer takes all the slack out of the system and puts the climber on belay.
4. The climber makes the transition over the edge (this can be very awkward), weights the anchor, and then clips a quickdraw to his or her harness and the belay rope below the anchor.
5. The belayer slowly lowers the climber down the route; because the climber is clipped to the rope between the protection bolt nearest the ground and the top anchor, he or she will be held in close to the rock and in line with the route—called tramming.
6. Each time a protection bolt is reached, the belayer locks off the belay and holds the climber.
7. The climber clips each bolt with a quickdraw and then clips the quickdraw to the rope just above where the quickdraw connected to his or her harness is clipped to the rope.

When the climber reaches the ground, the

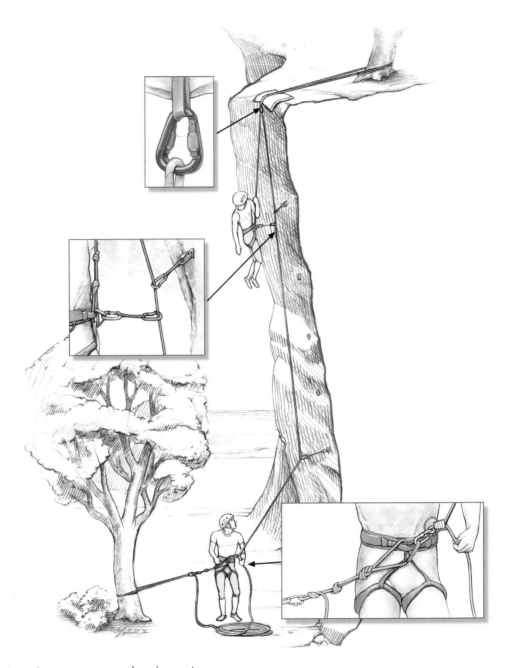

Setting up a top-rope on an overhanging route

rope should run from the belayer up through the quickdraws to the anchor and then back down to the climber. The first climber climbs up to the first bolt, unclips his or her rope from the quickdraw, and then clips the belay rope into the quickdraw—this helps the climber stay close to the rock as he or she is lowered later. As the climber continues up the route, he or she unclips the rope from each quickdraw as he or she comes to it. When the climber gets to the anchor, he or she clips a quickdraw between the harness and the rope below the anchor, and is lowered down, re-equipping the route for the next climber. The last climber to do the route cleans the quickdraws as he or she ascends, and then the anchor.

PULLING THE ROPE: WHAT IF IT GETS STUCK?

When the climbing is over, how do you get the rope down? If the top-rope has been set up from above, it is simple: Go back up and unclip the rope, then either drop it or pull it up, coil it, and carry it down. But what if the last climber was lowered or rappelled off? Theoretically it is still simple: Just pull the rope through the anchor. But sometimes this does not work and the rope gets stuck. If you do the following things, you will minimize the chance of getting your rope stuck.

1. Make sure that the last climber unties his or her tie-in knot completely, and do not pull the rope until you have made sure that there is no knot in the end. (It is quite common for each climber to leave the initial figure eight knot in the rope to make it easier for the next climber to tie in—do not do this if you are the last one down!)

2. Make sure that the rope is not being pulled through any cracks where it could jam, and position yourself well out from the cliff face or to the side when pulling the rope.

3. Pull the rope smoothly and slowly—jerking the rope or pulling too fast can cause the end to whip around and get jammed or even tie an overhand in itself before it gets to the anchor.

4. Continue to pull smoothly even after gravity has begun to pull the rope through the anchor—try to keep up with gravity as the rope falls; this helps minimize the possibility that the rope will jam a loop in a crack or get hung up on a ledge or projection.

Even when you are as careful as possible, the rope can still get hung up. What should you do? Most ropes will come down if tugged in the right direction. Step back, try to see what it is stuck on, and pull hard. If it does not come down and the anchor can be reached safely from above, go up and try to work it free from the top. If an extra rope is available, you can set up a rappel with a backup belay (see the autoblock belay in the Rappelling section of chapter 4, Retreat and an Introduction to Self-Rescue) and rappel the route to free the rope. If the rope is stuck just above the ground within safe bouldering distance, someone can climb up to it with a spot-check from below. Never try to climb the jammed rope; it could come loose unexpectedly with tragic results. If nothing works, leave the rope. You may be able to return later with someone who can help you retrieve it.

LEADING ON FIXED ANCHORS

The next logical step after you have mastered the systems for setting up safe top-ropes outdoors is to begin leading bolted (sport) routes. Sport climbing has grown by leaps and bounds over the last decade, and there are many climbing areas that consist almost exclusively of climbs with fixed protection and anchors. Leading sport climbs outside is a lot like leading them inside, with a few major differences:

- Real rock is not as friendly as plastic. It can be sharp, loose, wet, or dirty.
- Handholds are not always obvious and the moves can be hard to read.
- Not all falls outdoors are clean. There are ledges to bounce off, slabs to skid down, and other assorted hazards to avoid.
- On some routes, the rope may run over a sharp edge and the leader may need to use longer slings on the protection bolts to minimize the danger.
- There is no guarantee on the condition of the bolts, hangers, and top belay. There is no staff to monitor the placement or condition of any of the fixed equipment, and each bolt and anchor should be evaluated by the climber.
- The protection bolts may not be as close together as on lead routes in the gym, and they may not be positioned for easy clipping. Some routes may require supplemental protection; consult the guidebook or ask a local.
- You must clip the quickdraws to the protection bolts and then clip the rope in. That is twice as much clipping as indoors.
- When you reach the anchor, you must connect the slings to it—unlike the valet climbing at the gym, where all you do is clip the rope in and lower off.
- You must clean your own anchor and quickdraws when you are done.

Leading bolted routes outdoors requires judgment and diligence not usually needed indoors. Climbing outside should be challenging and fun; take care to do the following and you can concentrate on improving your skills and having a great time.

1. Be sure you are on your intended route. A lot of bolted routes look similar; be certain of your choice before you leave the ground.
2. Climb within your limits. Pushing your limits is fine, but trying a route three grades above your hardest is an invitation to frustration and injury.
3. Both the climber and the belayer should wear a helmet. The leader will be better protected and the belayer will be less likely to lose control of the belay if he or she is struck in the head by a rock.
4. Seriously consider having the belayer clipped to an anchor on the ground and use the **CATCH** principles described earlier in this chapter. This helps maximize the stability of the belayer and his or her ability to maintain control in the event of a hard leader fall.
5. Be sure that the belayer has the minimum amount of self-rescue equipment and knows how to escape the belay and assist the climber if necessary (see chapter 4, Retreat and an Introduction to Self-Rescue).
6. Make certain that the rope is stacked properly, with the climber's end coming off the top of the pile.
7. Be sure that both the climber's and the belayer's harnesses are on properly and the buckles are secure. Use the buddy check system.
8. Make sure the leader has enough quickdraws to complete the route—a good rule of thumb is one for each protection bolt, one for each anchor bolt, and one extra (in case one is dropped).

9. If the opening moves to the first bolt are difficult, have the belayer feed slack through the belay device and spot the leader until he or she makes the first clip. The belay will not be effective until then anyway, and you can save a sprained ankle, or worse; if spotting will not provide enough security, stick-clip the first bolt (clip the rope to a bolt by attaching a carabiner or quickdraw to a long stick).

10. While the leader is climbing, have the belayer watch out for any back clips (when the rope is clipped in such a way that during a fall it could cross over the carabiner's gate and accidentally open it) and warn the leader in time to correct the problem.

11. While belaying, be certain to keep the proper amount of slack in the system—just enough for the climber to move freely but not so much that he or she will fall farther than he or she should.

12. Be very careful when giving slack as the leader clips a protection bolt. Too much slack or slack too early means a longer fall if the leader misses the clip and falls; not enough slack or giving it too late means the climber will have to fight the rope to reach high enough for the clip, wasting energy and risking a fall during the clip. Always be ready to take the slack back in quickly if the leader misses the clip.

13. Stay alert while belaying. Do not get distracted watching other climbers or talking; a good belay is vital to a safe and successful lead.

14. When the leader reaches the anchor, do not let your guard down. Stay alert, keep the communication going, get confirmation before you act—"Are you sure I can take you off belay?"

15. Lower the climber slowly and smoothly, and pause at each bolt if the route is to be cleaned; if the climber is rappelling without an autoblock backup, give him or her a fireman's belay (see page 142) and hold the climber at each bolt if he or she is cleaning the route.

16. If the route is going to be top-roped after the lead, leave the necessary bolts clipped to minimize the swing potential.

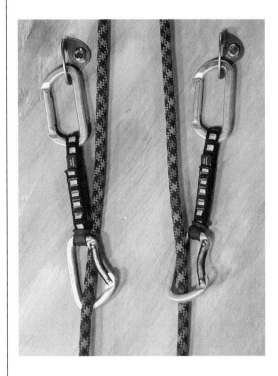

Beware the dreaded back clip: if the climber falls while climbing the strand on the left the rope may unclip itself from the carabiner. The rope should always run up the rock behind the carabiner and then come out through it to the climber; this way the rope will slide over the spine of the carabiner during a fall instead of over the gate.

CHAPTER 3

Traditional (Rock) Climbing

At the beginning of chapter 2, Sport Climbing Outdoors, we took our first step outside and learned how to top-rope and lead single-pitch climbs with fixed protection and anchors—the essence of "sport climbing." The next step is to examine the tools and techniques for climbing routes without any fixed gear—the essence of "traditional climbing."

Before sport climbing became popular, traditional climbing was all there was, and it was just called "rock climbing." Only after the sport-climbing rage took off in the late 1980s did the term "trad climbing" even come into existence. Up until then people became climbers by learning how to place protection and use all the tools to safely protect a lead and build an anchor. Today, it is not unusual to find highly skilled climbers—people who can climb really hard sport routes—who have never placed a nut in a crack.

There is danger in this. The transition from sport climbing to traditional climbing is even more complex than the transition from indoor climbing to sport climbing outdoors. With the high strength of today's fixed protection, most

beginning sport climbers can rely on the fixed protection they find at the crags and focus on doing the moves. Judgment is still needed, but the fundamental choices of how to protect a lead and build a top anchor have been made by someone else. The climber standing at the base of a long crack system with nothing but a guidebook and a rack of equipment will start making judgment calls before he or she leaves the ground, and will keep making decisions every step of the way while placing protection, building anchors, and belaying his or her partner. Safe traditional climbing depends on the proper use of a wide variety of equipment in complex systems. It takes time and experience to climb traditional routes safely.

But do not feel daunted; it is worth putting in the time to learn the systems. There are few greater satisfactions in rock climbing than leading a traditional pitch at your limit, protecting it well, and building a bombproof anchor at the top. Looking down the long line of protection points as your partner cleans the pitch is an immensely satisfying experience— perhaps more so than looking down a pitch of quickdraws on someone else's bolts. Also, when you have mastered the traditional climbing systems, a whole world of climbs opens up. You will no longer be limited to climbing only half a rope length off the ground.

This chapter looks at traditional rock climbing by working through the following progression:

- the equipment for traditional climbing
- how the various protection devices work
- top-roping single-pitch climbs using natural and constructed anchors
- leading single-pitch traditional climbs
- climbing multipitch traditional climbs

EQUIPMENT

Traditional climbing is very gear-intensive. A rack of quickdraws, a rope, and a harness do not cut it anymore. Climbers on traditional routes need to be prepared for anything, and this means carrying a lot of stuff. While the rack for an average sport climb may consist of

a dozen quickdraws and a couple of slings, it is not unusual for the trad climber to carry quickdraws, a dozen 24-inch slings, two cordelettes, twenty free carabiners, several locking carabiners, a nut pick, and twenty to thirty pieces of protection. Yes, it is heavy and sometimes cumbersome, and costs a lot of money! But the rewards are worth it. With the proper equipment and technique, you can leave the local sport crag behind and go anywhere and climb anything.

In chapter 1, Indoor Climbing—The Fundamentals, we discuss a lot of the basic safety equipment: carabiners, slings, quick-draws, belay/rappel devices, and helmets. For traditional climbing, we need to expand the list to include all the various types of protection as well as some specialized soft goods such as the cordelette.

CARABINERS

But first, let's go back for a moment and look at the most fundamental piece of hardware: the carabiner. Choosing a carabiner style used to be a simple question: Do you want Ds or ovals? But again, with the advent of sport climbing, the question has become more complicated. The market has been flooded with specially designed carabiners, most of which have been created to help sport climbers climb faster and lighter, and to make clips on desperate routes easier. Bent-gate carabiners, carabiners permanently attached to quickdraws, those with offset gates, or gates that are held open until the climber drops the rope into them, as well as ultralight carabiners that help shave precious ounces from the rack, all have their place—but that place is rarely on a traditional climb.

When you begin to build your "trad rack," stick to the basics. A rack full of the standard D and oval carabiners is a lot more versatile than a rack loaded with the latest "quick-clip-double-bent-string-gate-cyber-'biners." Basic carabiners are less expensive and better suited to most traditional-climbing situations. Some of the longest, hardest climbs in the world have been climbed without a single specialty carabiner.

PROTECTION

Protection is a generic term used for several types of devices that are carried by the climber and placed in the rock to provide temporary anchors. All protection devices carried by climbers are designed to work by wedging in cracks or holes in the rock. There are two fundamental ways to accomplish this: passively (no moving parts) or actively (moving parts).

A Note on Fixed Protection

Before the clean climbing revolution of the early '60s and '70s, climbers carried pitons—steel pegs of varying sizes that were driven into cracks with a hammer. Pitons were heavy, and their placement and removal scarred the rock. Where no other type of protection will work, pitons are still used today, and they are often

Whenever possible, back up a piton with a bombproof nut or cam.

found permanently in place for others to use. Pitons can be really secure, but using them requires extra caution. It is sometimes impossible to tell the age or condition of a piton left fixed in a crack. It may be bombproof. It may break under hand pressure. Go ahead and clip fixed pitons, but always back them up with another piece of protection whenever possible.

It is also quite common to find bolts on traditional climbs in places where the rock is blank and nothing else, including pitons, will work. Bolts are made of steel and are placed in holes drilled in the rock. They have a hanger with an eye in it to clip into. They come in many styles, are usually at least $3/8$ inch in diameter, and are tremendously strong when placed correctly in solid rock. Nonetheless, they should still be treated cautiously—there is no guarantee that they are sound. Clip them, but back them up whenever possible.

Passive Protection

Passive protection evolved from something found in nature: the chockstone. Early climbers occasionally found rocks wedged in cracks, and were delighted to discover that they could use them as protection by wrapping a piece of rope around them. But natural chockstones were not always around where they were needed.

One thing led to another, and soon climbers were carrying stones of various sizes around with them to wedge in cracks when they needed an anchor. Others climbers used machined nuts the same way. Eventually, entrepreneurs began making artificial chockstones out of metal and selling them; thus, "chocks" and "nuts" were born. The generic term *nut* is used in this book when referring to any type of passive protection. Today, several types of nuts are available:

- wedge-shaped nuts like Black Diamond Stoppers, Wild Country Rocks, DMM Wallnuts, HB Offsets, Trango Nutz, and Brassies
- hexoganal-shaped nuts like Black Diamond Hexentrics (an improvement by Yvon Chouinard on the machined nut design in which the opposite sides have a slight taper), Wild Country Rockcentrics, and Metolius Curve Hex-2000

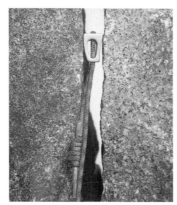

A good nut placement for a downward pull: the right side of the nut corresponds perfectly to the constriction and the left side has solid contact in the middle of its range. This placement would be even better if the constriction was such that the nut was equally strong for an outward pull.

A poor nut placement: the right side of the nut is barely contacting the rock and there is no obvious constriction. The left side of the nut is contacting the rock at the very top of its range. This placement would likely pull out in a fall.

This nut placement is strong for both downward and outward pull—it does not get much better than this.

A poor Tricam placement: The Tricam is too small for the crack, there is little holding the pivot point on the right side in place, and the left side is contacting the rock at the limit of its range. This placement would likely pull out during a fall.

A good Tricam placement: The pivot point is held securely in a depression in the rock and the left side has solid contact with the rock.

A good hex placement for a downward pull: the left side of the hex fits the slight constriction perfectly while the right side has solid contact in the middle of its range. A downward pull on the hex would cause it to attempt to rotate clockwise which would just wedge it tighter in the crack.

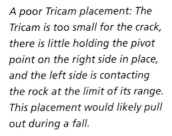

- other shapes, such as the Lowe Tricam, that use the camming principle to supplement their wedging action

Though the designs have changed over the years, they have not changed much and the various shapes based on the chockstone theme remain standard pieces of protection in the traditional climber's rack.

Active Protection

Passive protection is limited, however. All nuts rely on some type of constriction or irregularity in a crack for their holding power; they have to wedge against something. In the early clean climbing days in Yosemite National Park, where the cracks were often smooth and of uniform width, leaders were frequently unable to protect themselves adequately and had to "run it out" between good nut placements, risking long falls.

An answer to this puzzling problem was solved by Ray Jardine in the 1970s when he invented the first "Friend." Friends were the first successful spring-loaded camming devices (SLCDs, or "cams"), and though initially viewed with skepticism, they are now considered essential. SLCDs got around the need for a constriction or irregularity in the crack by using cams and simple physics. As force is applied to the shaft, the cams attempt to rotate around their axle. This increases the pressure between the cams and the rock, which also increases the holding power. When properly placed, an SLCD uses the angle of its cams against the rock to change the angle of a force from parallel to its shaft to just less than perpendicular—the same way a person can hold him or herself in place in a big chimney by spreading his or her feet wide apart. This clever design means that cams will work in any crack that has parallel, or even slightly flaring, sides.

Since the first Friends hit the market more

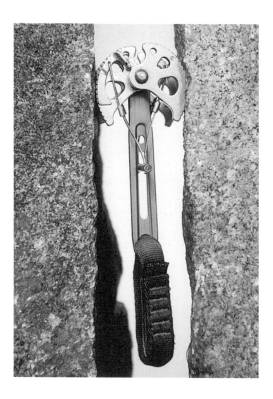

A perfect SLCD placement has each cam in solid contact with the rock near the middle of the expansion range.

The top SLCD in this photo is over-cammed and though it may be secure, it may also be extremely difficult to remove; the lower SLCD is under-cammed causing it to be unstable and it may not hold a fall.

than two decades ago, many variations on the design have been made. SLCDs with four cams, three cams, cams of different widths, rigid stems, flexible stems, single cam axles, double cam axles, and more are all available. SLCDs fit cracks ranging from narrower than a pinkie to nearly big enough to crawl into, and are considered indispensable on many climbs.

SLCDs are functional, flashy, and usually simple to place; however, a note of caution is in order. SLCDs are not magic. They only work when properly placed, and that takes understanding and judgment. Just shoving them into a crack guarantees nothing. Resist the temptation to rely on them at the expense of other forms of protection. Just because they have springs and moving parts does not mean that they are better than passive nuts. In fact, nuts often provide more secure placements in cracks than SLCDs. Carry a variety of passive and active devices, analyze each placement, and pick the very best piece of protection for each circumstance.

In addition to the nuts and standard SLCDs, there are specialty devices designed to meet a particular need. There are spring-loaded, telescoping tubes; oversize SLCDs for protecting offwidth cracks; and other esoteric devices that will occasionally be needed. But for the beginning trad climber, stick to the basics. If a climb calls for specialized gear, it is usually mentioned in the route description. The trick then is to borrow the specialized stuff from a friend so you can save your money for some more standard carabiners.

Wide crack protection can take the form of the Trango Big Bro, an expanding tube or . . .

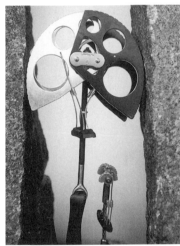

. . . any number of designs of oversized SLCD's like this huge Black Diamond Camelot. A cam designed to fit a 1-inch crack is pictured below this cam for comparison.

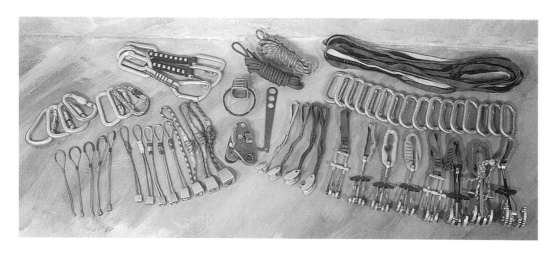

A standard rack that will work in most areas includes a wide selection of passive and active protection as well as slings, quickdraws, cordelettes, locking and non-locking carabiners, a belay/rappel device, and a nut pick.

THE RACK

Besides a selection of nuts and cams, the traditional climber will need to carry several other pieces of hardware:

- nut pick—a long, thin, metal pick with a keeper cord that is used to poke and pull on nuts to aid in their removal; one should be carried by each climber
- cordelette—a 6- to 10-foot loop of cord made of 7 mm perlon, 5.5 mm Spectra cord, or other similar materials that is used to build anchors and is incorporated into some self-rescue systems; usually two cordelettes are carried by the leader
- slings—usually $9/16$-inch material tied or sewn in loops from 4 inches to 48 inches in length that are used to make connections between parts in the system; the shorter sizes are used for quickdraws, six to ten 24-inch slings are helpful on many pitches, and a couple of 48-inch slings are useful for building belay anchors

Exactly what equipment a climber will need depends on the climb. A one-pitch, straight-up hand crack may not require lots of slings, tiny nuts, or big cams, while a long multipitch route in Yosemite National Park might require all the gear from the racks of two climbers. Guidebooks often give advice on what gear to bring and in what sizes, or you can ask others who have done the route for their suggestions. On many routes, it is obvious by looking at them what you will need. But even with the best information, it is wise to err on the side of caution, bringing more than you think you might need. Minimal racks are for people who know for sure that they will not get in trouble, but the consequences can be disastrous when they are wrong. A standard rack that works on most climbs in most areas consists of:

a set of micro-nuts to cover cracks from $1/8$ inch to $1/2$ inch

a set of standard nuts to cover cracks from $1/2$ inch to $1 1/2$ inches

a selection of cams to cover from $^1/_2$ inch to 3
  inches (hexagonal or cam-shaped passive
  protection can be included for variety)
several quickdraws
six to ten 2-foot sewn slings
nut pick
several locking carabiners
nonlocking carabiners to carry the protection
twelve to eighteen free nonlocking
  carabiners
belay/rappel device (a spare is always a
  good idea)
two cordelettes (optional)

BELAY ANCHORS

USING SIMPLE, NATURAL ANCHORS

The first step in traditional climbing is learning
how to set up top-ropes on climbs without fixed
top anchors. Understanding how to build simple
anchors using natural protection points allows
you to climb at many areas without fixed
anchors. The most common natural anchors are
trees and boulders. Below is a suggested equipment list for building simple, natural anchors:

twelve oval or D nonlocking carabiners
at least three locking carabiners
six 24-inch sewn slings
two 48-inch sewn slings
two 6 mm by 24-inch prusik loops
one 10-foot knotted sling made of 1-inch
  tubular webbing
one 15-foot knotted sling made of 1-inch
  tubular webbing
one 20-foot knotted sling made of 1-inch
  tubular webbing
an extra rope (for areas where the anchor
  points are way back from the edge)
materials for padding the cliff edge
Next we look at how to construct simple,

natural anchors using a single large tree or
block near the edge, or multiple trees or blocks
near the edge, which might require use of a
second rope. Instructions for building these
belay anchors follow this principle: All top-
rope anchors must be **SECURE.** You can be a
5.13 climber or the world's greatest belayer, but
if your anchor is not **SECURE** you are risking
your life.

S—The anchor is *strong* enough.
E—The master point is *extended* over the edge.
C—The master point is *centered* over the
  climb.
U—The master point consists of an *unbroken*
  ring of metal.
R—The rope *runs* easily.
E—The *edge* is padded when necessary.

Strong. Is the anchor(s) you have chosen
strong enough? Trees should be at least 6 inches
in diameter, alive, well rooted (trees growing on
cliffs are notoriously shallow-rooted), and stable.
Boulders and blocks should be really big, free of
sharp edges, stable, and positioned so they
cannot slip. If you are considering just one tree
or boulder, is it really strong enough to be used
by itself? Err on the conservative side. If there is
any doubt, look for an additional anchor.

Extended. Arrange the anchor so the master
point is extended over the edge of the cliff. The
master point is the main attachment point in a
belay anchor—the point where all the individual anchor components come together. In a
top-rope anchor, the master point usually
consists of two carabiners that are opposed and
reversed (see Unbroken, below). If you do not
extend the master point over the edge of the
cliff, the rope will be forced to run up and over
the edge and back down again; it will not run
easily, and you risk cutting it (ropes cut
alarmingly easily under tension, even over the
most benign-appearing edges).

*A **SECURE** top-rope anchor is **S**trong, **E**xtends over the edge, is **C**entered over the route, the master point is an **U**nbroken ring of metal, the rope **R**uns easily, and the **E**dge is padded as needed. In this case the left side of the anchor is padded with 1-inch tubular webbing and the sling on the right is padded with a length of garden hose.*

Centered. Be certain the master point is centered over the climb to minimize the climber's potential swing. If the climb traverses (making it impossible to center the rope), then intermediate anchors will need to be placed along the route, probably on rappel—this complicates the setup considerably and unless you are confident in your ability to set up the top-rope safely, you should choose another route.

Unbroken. The master point must be constructed so an unbroken ring of metal is created. Use a minimum of two carabiners with their gates reversed and opposed to form a ring of metal as your master point. Single carabiners, whether locking or not, or multiple carabiners with their gates aligned the same

way, can and do fail by coming unclipped. To set up carabiners reversed and opposed, clip them in from opposite directions (for example, one from the right, one from the left), so they form an X when their gates are both open, and then spin one around so that the gates are on opposite sides. Use two locking carabiners for extra security. Never compromise this principle.

Run. The rope must run easily in order to ensure a safe belay. After you have determined that your anchor is strong, extended over the edge, and centered over the route, and you have created an unbroken master point, clip the rope in and test it to see if it will run freely. Make whatever adjustments necessary to the system to ensure this. The rope must run freely to provide a proper belay.

Edge. If you do everything correctly up to this point but fail to protect the edge, you have failed to create a **SECURE** anchor. Be quick to pad edges, even if they look fine. It does not

Edging adding options include: running the rope through 1-inch tubular webbing, sliding on a piece of garden hose (split lengthwise), or . . .

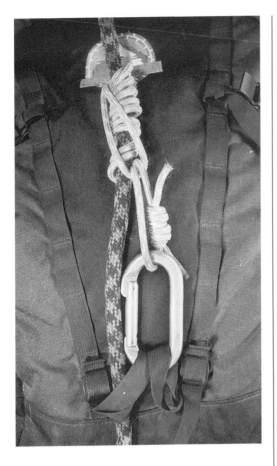

. . . using a pack held in place with a Klemheist or prusik sling clipped in with a carabiner.

take much to abrade a rope or sling—even rough rock without an obvious edge can be dangerous! Padding options include backpacks, clothing, 1-inch tubular webbing, or lengths of old garden hose or fire hose.

Single Tree or Boulder

Trees make wonderful anchors, and it is a great day when you find a huge oak positioned perfectly over the climb, with roots buried deep in bedrock. But be careful with trees—looks can be deceiving. Before you use a tree as an anchor, be sure that it is:

- alive—dead trees lose strength quickly as they rot or dry out
- well anchored—trees growing on cliffs are often rooted in shallow pads of forest duff, and even big trees can be unstable; look for roots extending down into rock
- big enough—6 inches is a good minimum size for use as a single-point anchor; smaller trees can be tied together in a multipoint anchor (described in the next section)

Boulders can also make great anchors, but they require extensive evaluation. Before you use a boulder as an anchor, check to see whether it is:

- big enough—since boulders are not anchored by roots like trees, they must be big to be secure; 3 feet square is a good minimum
- stable—even really big boulders can be unstable; check to be sure it cannot be rolled, slid, or tipped; if you have any doubts, pick another anchor
- sharp-edged—be absolutely sure that no edge will damage the sling or rope that is wrapped around the boulder; pad edges as necessary
- the right shape to hold the sling or rope— slings cannot slip off trees, but they sure can slip off rocks; when you wrap the sling around the boulder, analyze the direction of pull and be absolutely sure that the sling will stay in place; if in doubt, use other anchors to hold the main anchor in place, or pick another main anchor

If you determine that a single tree or boulder will create a strong-enough anchor, the only question is how to tie it off. A girth-

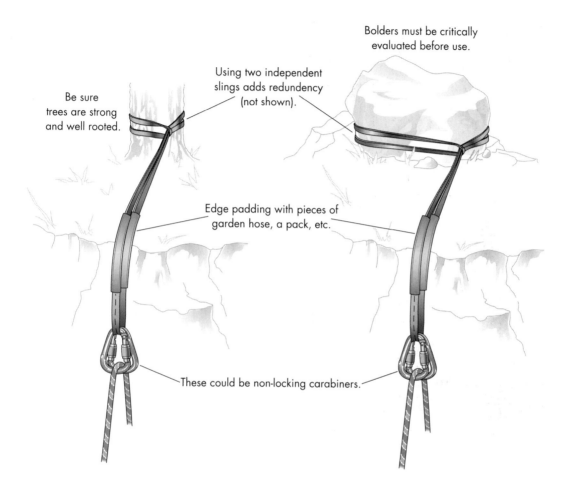

Bolders must be critically evaluated before use.

Using two independent slings adds redundency (not shown).

Be sure trees are strong and well rooted.

Edge padding with pieces of garden hose, a pack, etc.

These could be non-locking carabiners.

Using slings to create an anchor from a single tree or boulder. Always consider padding edges. Master points should consist of at least two carabiners reversed and opposed—they don't have to be locking.

hitched sling is the easiest method. If necessary, several slings can be girth-hitched together to extend the anchor over the edge. Remember to adhere to all the **SECURE** principles. When relying on a single anchor, it is always a good idea to double up all the slings to build redundancy into the system. Use good judgment when girth-hitching slings to trees, and consider leverage. If the tree is big, feel free to girth-hitch it at whatever height off the ground will make the anchor most effective. If the tree is small or you are at all concerned with leverage, girth-hitch it as close to the ground as possible.

A sling girth-hitched around a stout tree can make a solid single-point top-rope anchor—a second sling adds redundancy and peace of mind.

Multiple Trees or Boulders

There are several options for creating a top-rope belay using two or more natural anchors such as trees. Learning the fundamentals in the following systems will build a base of knowledge and allow you to safely innovate when circumstances demand.

Slings: Using slings long enough to extend over the edge of the cliff, girth-hitch one to each tree or boulder, bring the ends together, and clip in your carabiners to create the master point (remember to always tie in to

something when working near the edge of a cliff). If you are fortunate, the slings will center themselves over the route and they will be equalized.

If one of the slings is longer than the other, the system can still be equalized by clipping a carabiner to the shorter sling, clipping the longer sling into it, and then creating a magic X in the longer sling. Alternatively, a third

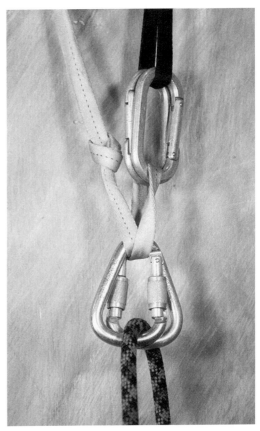

Another method creates a magic X between the two slings. An overhand knot has been tied in the longer sling to reduce the potential extension.

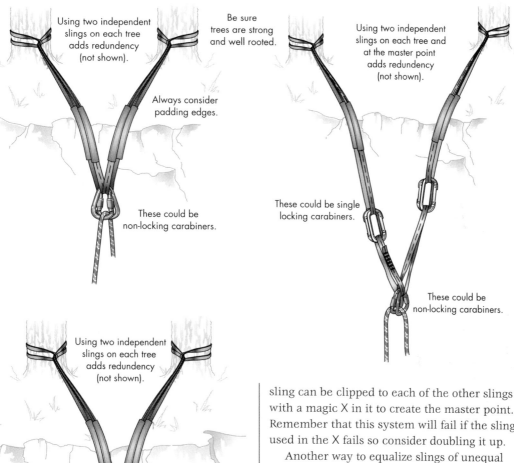

Using two independent slings on each tree adds redundancy (not shown).

Be sure trees are strong and well rooted.

Always consider padding edges.

These could be non-locking carabiners.

Using two independent slings on each tree and at the master point adds redundancy (not shown).

These could be single locking carabiners.

These could be non-locking carabiners.

Using two independent slings on each tree adds redundancy (not shown).

These could be non-locking carabiners.

Use an overhand on a bight to shorten a sling

Three methods for tying two natural anchors together

sling can be clipped to each of the other slings with a magic X in it to create the master point. Remember that this system will fail if the sling used in the X fails so consider doubling it up.

Another way to equalize slings of unequal lengths is to simply tie an overhand on a bight in the long sling at the same level as the end of the short sling—effectively making both slings the same length. When the overhand knot is loaded, it will attempt to pull apart—do not worry; just tie the overhand neatly and tighten it well, and there will be no problem.

Separate climbing rope: If the anchors are too far from the edge for slings, a spare climbing rope can easily be used to form your anchor. One simple way to equalize this system with trees is to use a friction wrap.

First, tie the end of the rope to the first tree using a figure eight on a bight with a double fisherman backup knot. (To protect yourself while working near the edge, wrap a sling around the rope using a Klemheist or prusik hitch and clip it to your harness with a locking carabiner; see chapter 4, Retreat and an Introduction to Self-Rescue, for more information on using these hitches. Slide the sling up and down the rope as you move about while setting up the system.) Next run the rope down to the edge and tie in a figure eight on a bight master-point loop. Now run the free end of the rope back up to the second anchor and wrap the rope around the tree four to six times. Finally, tie a figure eight on a bight loop in the rope and clip it back into the rope between the second tree and the master point with either a locking carabiner or two carabiners reversed and opposed—this closes the system.

Using a Klemheist hitch on the rope allows the climber to move freely and safely while setting up a top-rope next to the edge of a cliff. Note the climber's figure eight backup knot as well.

If the anchors consist of two boulders, a good way to equalize them is to use slings or cordelettes to tie off each boulder. Clip one end of the spare climbing rope into the sling on one boulder with a figure eight on a bight with a double fisherman backup knot and either a locking carabiner or two carabiners reversed and opposed, tie the master-point figure eight at the edge of the cliff, and then run the rope up to the sling on the second boulder and clip it in with another figure eight on a bight using a locking carabiner or two carabiners reversed and opposed. You can fine-tune the position of

the master point by feeding rope either in or out of the anchor knots.

If the anchor consists of three independent points that are far enough apart to require using a separate rope, then the following setup works well if it is three trees: Girth-hitch each tree with a sling. Tie a figure eight on a bight with a double fisherman backup knot into one end of the rope and clip it to the first anchor. Run the rope down to the edge, then back up, and clip it through the sling on the middle anchor, then back down to the edge, and finally back up to the third anchor and clip it in with a

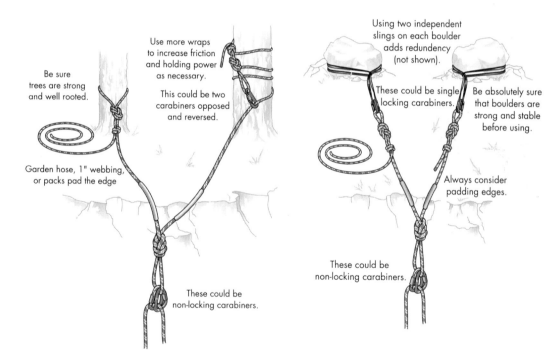

Using two trees and a friction wrap to create a top-rope anchor

Using slings to create an equalized anchor on two boulders

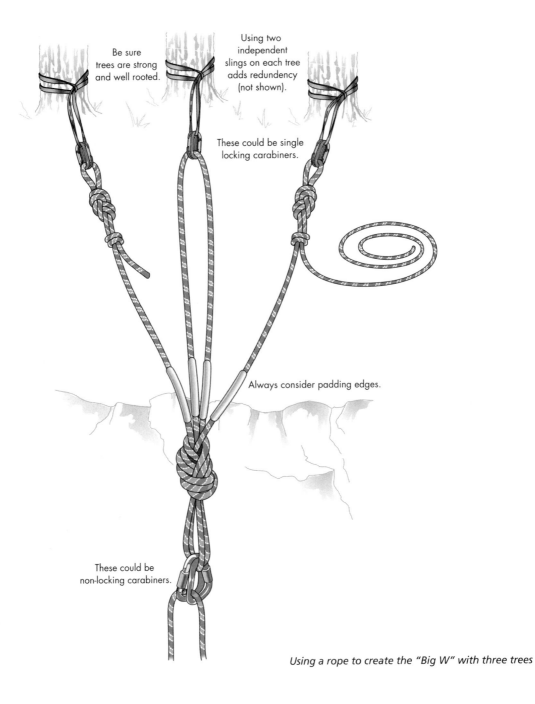

Be sure trees are strong and well rooted.

Using two independent slings on each tree adds redundancy (not shown).

These could be single locking carabiners.

Always consider padding edges.

These could be non-locking carabiners.

Using a rope to create the "Big W" with three trees

figure eight on a bight. You should now have a big W of rope. Now go back to the edge, equalize the two bottom legs of the W, and tie a figure eight on a bight using all four strands of the rope for the master point. If the master point is not in the right position, untie the master point, untie the figure eight on the third anchor, take in or feed out rope as needed, retie the figure eight, and then retie the master point. This system equalizes each point, allows great latitude in the position of the final anchor, and creates a double-strand master point—bombproof!

On any of these top-rope setups, if the master point will be in contact with the rock while the rope is belayed through it, consider building redundancy into the system. If you built the belay using slings, consider doubling up the slings that form the master point. If you built the belay using a second rope, consider building a second figure eight on a bight.

USING CONSTRUCTED ANCHORS

Trees and boulders can only take you so far. Some climbs just do not have natural anchors conveniently located above them. Now it is time to take that trad rack loaded with passive and active protection, and learn to construct anchors. Anchors that are made of gear you place yourself need to be **ERNEST:**

- **E—** All anchor points should be *equalized.*
- **R—** The anchor must be *redundant,* consisting of multiple points.
- **NE—**There should be *no extension* if one anchor in the system fails.
- **S—** Each anchor point must be *strong* and *stable.*
- **T—** The anchor must be *timely,* that is, correctly positioned.

Equalized. A good traditional anchor has all

Tying two figure eight loops creates redundancy at the master point.

of the individual protection points sharing the load as equally as possible. Stringing protection points in a line wherein only one carries the load can create a dangerous "zipper effect" that disintegrates the entire belay.

Redundant. All belay anchors (with the exception of big trees, huge boulders, et cetera) must consist of more than one anchor point. In solid rock with cracks perfectly suited to nut and cam placement, you may be able to build an anchor using just two pieces of protection.

KEY TRANSITION EXERCISE: LEARNING THE VITAL SKILLS FOR CLIMBING OUTSIDE
Using Natural Anchor Points to Create a Secure Top-Rope Belay Anchor

THE CHALLENGE
Building great top-rope anchors outdoors can be complicated, the process itself can be dangerous, and the end result is not always as safe as it can be.

THE DIFFERENCE BETWEEN USING NATURAL ANCHOR POINTS INDOORS AND OUTDOORS
Indoors: You do not build top-rope anchors indoors. The top-ropes are permanently in place.
Outdoors: Top-roping outdoors always involves building an anchor. It can be as easy as clipping a pair of quickdraws to bolts, or as complex as tying multiple, distant anchor points together on an exposed and dangerous edge.

THE GOAL
Master tie-off methods, creating safe, **SECURE** top-rope belay anchors using natural anchor points.

THE EQUIPMENT
> 1 rope
> 1–2 cordelettes
> 2 locking carabiners
> 1 backpack
> 6–8 2-foot slings
> 6 nonlocking carabiners
> 3 natural anchors (trees, posts, et cetera)
> 1 simulated edge (crate, box, bench, et cetera)
> 1 backpack
> 18-inch lengths of garden hose (split) and 1-inch tubular webbing

THE SETUP
Find a place where three trees or similar anchor points exist within approximately 15 feet of each other.

The Natural Anchor Points Exercise
First, here is a review of the **SECURE** principles:
S—The anchor is *strong* enough.
E—The master point is *extended* over the edge.
C—The master point is *centered* over the climb.
U—The master point consists of an *unbroken* ring of metal.
R—The rope *runs* easily.
E—The *edge* is padded when necessary.

The three options below are designed to introduce you to many different techniques that can be used in various combinations to create **SECURE** top-rope anchors—the possible combinations are limited only by your imagination!

Slings and Cordelettes

1. Place the simulated edge in front of two anchor points.
2. Girth-hitch the first anchor with a sling or cordelette and then add girth-hitched slings to reach over the edge.
3. Tie an overhand loop in the end (this closes the system and ensures that if the last sling in the chain has one of its strands cut, the sling will not fail) .
4. Duplicate step 2 on the second anchor.
5. Clip the overhand loops together with two reversed and opposed, locking carabiners to form the master point, and thread the climbing rope through it.
6. Girth-hitch a sling through the grab loop on the backpack (or any other convenient attachment point) and clip the other end in to the appropriate loop on one of the anchor slings so that the pack will stay under the slings and over the edge—practicing how to pad an edge can save your life, so do not ever skip this if the edge is at all suspect!

The Rope and a Friction Wrap

1. Tie the end of the rope around the first anchor using a figure eight follow-through and keeper knot.
2. Run the rope down over the simulated edge and tie a figure eight loop as the master point.
3. Run the rope up to the second anchor, wrap the rope around it three to five times (more wraps are needed on a tree with a small diameter), tie an overhand loop, and clip it back to the rope with a pair of reversed and opposed, nonlocking carabiners or a locking carabiner.
4. Check that the master point is positioned over the edge correctly and adjust the friction-wrap loops as necessary.
5. Clip a pair of reversed and opposed, locking carabiners to the master point.
6. For edge protection use 18-inch lengths of garden hose split lengthwise and slipped over the rope, or prethread the rope through two 18-inch lengths of 1-inch tubular webbing, and position one on the rope on each side of the master point.

The "Big W" Method Using Three Anchors and the Rope

1. Girth-hitch a sling around each tree.
2. Tie a figure eight loop in the end of the rope (leave long tails) and clip it to the sling on the first tree with a locking carabiner or a pair of reversed and opposed, nonlocking carabiners.
3. Run the rope down over the simulated edge and then back up to the second tree.
4. Tie a figure eight loop in the rope and clip it to the sling.

5. Run the rope back down over the edge (it should hang over just as far as the first loop), then back up to the third tree.
6. Tie another figure eight loop and clip it in to the third sling.
7. Lay the two loops over the edge on top of each other, tie a figure eight on a bight to form the master point, and clip in the master-point carabiners.
8. Pad the edge using a pack, garden hose, or webbing.

In crumbly rock with funky cracks, you may put in a half dozen or more. How many pieces to use is a matter of judgment, and is different for each belay anchor. Make it a top priority to learn how to place gear securely, and always err on the side of too many pieces instead of too few. The end result must be an anchor that you trust completely.

No Extension. Shock loading any system can be dangerous. Whenever possible, eliminate the possibility that the system may "extend" if any one component fails. The classic example is a magic X anchor wherein one of the anchor points pulls out—the system extends until the second point takes the load. Extension can be minimized in a magic X system by tying an overhand knot in the sling on each side of the anchor. (A word of reassurance regarding the magic X: Though the system has the potential to extend, the anchors almost never fail; use the magic X with confidence any time you need to equalize two good anchor points.)

Strong and **Stable.** Each nut or cam must be placed in the most secure position possible, be aligned with the anticipated load, and be stable. Weak placements that are out of line and wobbly should never be trusted.

Timely. Belay anchors need to be built in the right place. This principle is specifically for multipitch climbing wherein the leader must decide when and where to belay—if too far away from the second climber, vital visual and verbal communication may be impossible.

Remember, after you have created an **ERNEST** top-rope anchor, check it to be sure it is also **SECURE:** *strong* enough, the master point *extended* over the edge, *centered* over the climb, consisting of an *unbroken* ring of metal, through which the rope *runs* easily, and the *edge* is padded if necessary.

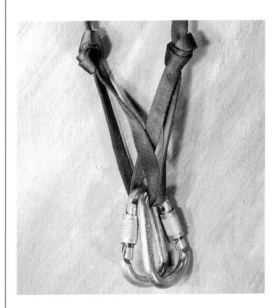

You can minimize the possibility of extension in a magic X anchor by tying overhand knots in the sling above the master point.

KEY TRANSITION EXERCISE: LEARNING THE VITAL SKILLS FOR CLIMBING OUTSIDE
Constructing Belay Anchors Using Traditional Protection

THE CHALLENGE

When natural anchors are not available, an anchor must be constructed using the gear the climber carries. Excellent technical skills and good judgment are mandatory for such anchors to be effective and reliable. It is too easy to build bad anchors!

THE DIFFERENCE BETWEEN CONSTRUCTING ANCHORS INDOORS AND OUTDOORS

Indoors: You never have to construct anchors indoors.
Outdoors: Anchors must be constructed outdoors anytime that fixed or natural anchors do not exist.

THE GOAL

Learn and master the various ways to tie protection points together into a belay anchor using the equipment carried by the climber.

THE EQUIPMENT

    1 rope
    1 cordelette
    2 locking carabiners
    4–6 2-foot slings
    6 nonlocking carabiners
    1 standard climbing rack (at least one set each of nuts and cams)

THE SETUP

This exercise cannot be done in your backyard unless you are blessed with a cliff or boulders on your property. The base of a cliff with lots of cracks is the best place to go. Be sure that the area is safe (do not practice this at the edge of the top of a cliff or at an area where spontaneous or climber-generated rockfall would make the base area dangerous).

    Note: This exercise does not describe how to place solid individual anchor points. Though the photos and captions in this book will help you understand the fundamental principles, they will not make you an expert. If you are inexperienced at placing protection, it is highly recommended that you take an anchoring class with a professional instructor or ask an expert friend to accompany you on this exercise. Constructed anchors can look fine, but they are only as strong as the individual placements. Do not build a false sense of security; get an expert critique before you leave the ground.

The Constructed Belay Exercise

A constructed belay can be as simple as tying two bomber pieces together using a magic X or as complex as connecting a half dozen nuts of varying individual security. This exercise focuses on two things: the magic X system, and using a cordelette to tie multiple pieces together. Whenever possible, remember to make your anchor in accordance with the **ERNEST** principles:

E—The individual anchor points are *equalized*.

R—The anchor is *redundant*—there are at least two trustworthy pieces.

NE—There will be *no extension* (shock load) if an individual point fails.

S—Each anchor point is as *strong* and *stable* as possible.

T—The anchor is *timely* (in the right place).

As in the Key Transition Exercise that covered Using Natural Anchor Points to Create a Secure Top-Rope Belay, this exercise is designed to introduce the basic principles and practice the standard systems. The magic X and the cordelette system can be integrated and again, the climber's imagination is the only limiting factor.

Tying Two Points Using the Magic X

The first option ties two pieces together using a sling and the magic X. The magic X is the simplest method used to tie two anchor points together. Assuming that each point is strong and stable, and that the belay is being built in the right place, the magic X anchor meets all the criteria for being **ERNEST,** except one: If an anchor point fails, there will be some *extension* as the magic X slides and the second point will be shock loaded. Nonetheless, the magic X system is extremely

A simple two-point constructed anchor equalized with a sling and a magic X can be minimized by tying overhand knots above the master point on either side of the sling. A second sling placed the same as the first would make the anchor sling redundant and add security.

useful, and by using good anchoring skills and judgment, the risk of shock-loading the system is extremely remote.

1. Place two solid anchor points no more than a foot or so apart.
2. Take a 24-inch sling and clip it to each anchor point with a nonlocking carabiner (to build in more redundancy, consider using two slings instead of one).
3. Pull both strands of the sling down so they lie on top of each other.
4. Put a 180-degree twist in either strand, forming a loop.
5. Clip a locking carabiner through the loop and over the other strand, forming the master point.
6. Unclip either protection point and allow the system to extend—if you have done it right, the system will catch again; if not, then the master-point carabiner will slide off the sling—a sobering moment.

Note: The extension can be minimized by tying an overhand loop on each side of the sling above the master point, and it can be eliminated if two independent slings are used.

Tying Three Points Using the Magic X

1. Place three anchor points within a foot or so of each other.
2. Create a magic X between the first and second point and clip in with a nonlocking carabiner, creating a sub-master point.
3. Create a magic X between the second and third point and clip in with a nonlocking carabiner, creating a second sub-master point.

Three points connected with multiple magic Xs. This is effective but gear intensive, and the setup will extend if any one point fails.

4. Create a magic X between the two sub-master points and clip in with a locking carabiner to create the final master point.

Note: The above system places equal weight on each of the three anchor points. It can be simplified by creating a magic X between the first sub-master point and the third point. This splits the load as follows: 25 percent each on points one and two, 50 percent on point three. There are no limitations on the number of anchor points that can be tied together using the magic X system. However, after three individual anchor points, the system becomes very gear-intensive and cumbersome. The cordelette system in the next option is far superior for tying together multiple anchor points.

Tying Multiple Pieces Together Using a Cordelette

The cordelette should be considered an indispensable tool. It is incredibly useful for building belay anchors, and doubles as a key component in many self-rescue systems. The cordelette has been a standard piece of equipment used by professional guides for more than a decade, and is becoming more and more popular with recreational climbers.

1. Place three anchor points a foot or so apart.
2. Clip the cordelette to each point with a nonlocking carabiner (place the knot in the cordelette between two of the anchor points—this will keep it from becoming entangled in the master point later).
3. Grasp the strand of the cordelette between points one and two with one hand and between points two and three with the other, and pull them down until they meet the big loop hanging down below—three loops will form in the process.
4. Work the three loops back and forth until all the slack is out of the system, pre-equalize them in the direction the anchor will be stressed, and carefully tie an overhand or figure eight loop to form the master point.
5. Weight the system and be sure that each of the three loops is equally stressed—rearrange the loops and retie the master point loop as necessary to equalize the system.

Note: Using a cordelette creates three independent, full-strength loops—one between each anchor point and the master point. If any one of these loops fails, there will be no

*The first step in creating an **ERNEST** anchor using a cordelette is to place three solid, strong anchors; clip the cordelette through each one; and then pull down the three loops.*

extension in the system. This is one of the simplest and most secure methods of creating an **ERNEST** anchor. The same system can be used to equalize up to four individual anchor points. More than that, and most cordelettes are simply not long enough to make the connections.

A final, extremely important note. Any anchor that will be used to belay a leader *must* be built so the belayer cannot be pulled upward if the leader falls. The belay should be built with one or more bombproof pieces that are oriented for an upward pull clipped to the master point. This makes the belay anchor multidirectional. In addition, the belayer should clip a separate sling from the harness to these upward-oriented points. This will keep the belayer from being pulled upward during a hard leader fall.

Pre-equalize the three loops in the direction that you anticipate them being loaded, and tie a figure eight or overhand on a bight to form the master point.

This cordelette anchor can be used as a belay anchor for a leader because a piece has been placed for an upward pull and clipped to the mas-ter point with a quickdraw.

This climber is well prepared to belay a leader. Both the anchor and the belayer are protected from an upward pull by an anchor point below that will hold that force.

OUTSIDE MOVES

CRACK CLIMBING

If there is one thing that climbing gyms do not do well (yet), it is giving people a chance to climb cracks. Climb a lot in the gym, and you may get really good at overhanging sport routes, but you may be stopped cold by a 5.8 hand crack. Crack climbing is very different from the typical face climbing found in most gyms and on most sport routes, primarily because there are not any "holds."

Climbing cracks depends on jamming fingers, hands, feet, even elbows securely in a crack without holding onto anything. Crack climbing can be as brutally obvious as a 2-inch fissure running for hundreds of feet in desert sandstone or as devious and delicate as discontinuous fingertip fractures up a smooth granite slab. Cracks can offer easy progress or offer some of the most strenuous and technically difficult climbing imaginable. Crack climbing techniques can be broken down by approximate size:

1/4 inch to 1 inch	finger cracks
1 inch to 3 inches	hand cracks
3 inches to 5 inches	fist cracks
5 inches to 10 inches	offwidth cracks
10 inches and larger	chimney cracks

Using your feet well is the key to making any crack less strenuous. As soon as a crack is wide enough to accept your toe, it can be used as a foothold. Look for wide places in the crack where you can jam your foot straight in. If the crack is thin, turn the inside of your ankle up, stick your toe in sideways, torque hard, and stand up. On really thin cracks, look for any irregularity, offset, or possible foothold on the edge of the crack to stand on.

Finger Cracks

For many people, finger cracks feel the most natural—jamming your fingers in a crack is not that far from crimping on a face hold. A secure finger jam is made when a knuckle wedges into a constriction in the crack, much the same way that you jam a nut. If the crack is thin or shallow, you may only be able to jam a fingertip. These "tips" cracks offer strenuous and insecure jamming, and often feel more like face climbing than crack climbing. Wider and deeper cracks allow you to bury your fingers and jam a knuckle. Spending time "working" the jam will often make it better. Cracks that allow you to jam back to the second set of knuckles can be really secure. Security comes with a price, however. Finger cracks are too small to allow you to jam your toes in as well, so if there are not accompanying edges for your feet, finger cracks can be very strenuous and often painful.

When climbing finger cracks—and hand cracks as well—you must decide whether a jam should be made with the thumb up or down. Thumb-up jams allow for greater reach between jams, but are often less secure than thumb-down jams, which are improved by the camming action of the hand position. Many jams will dictate thumb up or thumb down on their own; one way will feel solid and secure and the other will not. On many climbs, a thumb-down position on the top jam and a thumb-up position on the lower jam is most efficient. This position allows the body to lean to one side of the crack, often adding security to the jams and making it easier for the toes to get a grip on the edge of the crack. This works especially well on cracks that lean. Keep your body on the downhill side, thumb down on top, thumb up on the bottom, use one foot on the edge of the crack and the other on face holds or smearing below the crack. Progress is either made by shuffling your hands up or crossing one over the other—whichever feels most efficient and secure.

One of the most difficult crack sizes is called "off fingers." While this size will vary depending on the finger size of the climber, it is always unpleasant to find yourself jamming a crack that is too wide for your fingers but too narrow for your hands. Jams in these cracks are often "rattly," and security can be increased by making them thumb down, torquing hard, and, in some cases, opposing a thumb against the side of the crack.

Hand Cracks

Once they are accustomed to hand cracks, many people find them to be their favorite crack size. A good hand jam can be as secure as a jug hold and is often less strenuous to hold

The classic thumb-down finger jam utilizes a camming action to improve security.

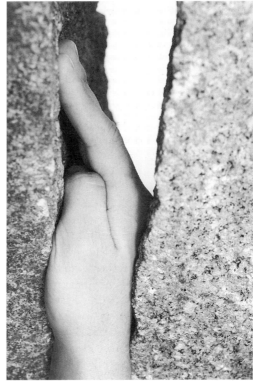

A good hand jam can be better than a bucket.

onto. A good hand jam grabs the flesh just above the wrist and holds it so firmly that all you have to do is hang from it—little muscle-flexing is required. And hand cracks often make great footholds, which can also ease the strenuousness.

A hand jam is a remarkably simple thing. Insert your hand into a crack, just above a constriction if possible, work it until it seats, then tuck your thumb into your palm and squeeze. The better the constriction and the harder you squeeze, the more secure the jam will be. A really good hand jam will go in easily and painlessly, and feel so secure you would swear you could belay off it. As with finger jams, the thumb-up or -down decision will have to be made with each jam. A thumb-down upper jam and thumb-up lower jam is often the best combination.

Thin hand cracks and off-hand cracks offer complications similar to those of tips and off-finger cracks. Thin hand cracks allow the knuckles on the back of your hand but not the flesh of your hand or a place to tuck your thumb. Placing the thumb down, torquing hard, and moving quickly are keys to using these jams effectively. Off-hand cracks are so wide that no matter how hard you tuck your thumb, torque, and squeeze, the jam feels terrible. Take as much weight off your hands as possible by using your feet well, and move fast.

Fist Cracks

When cracks get wider than hands, they get annoyingly difficult because hands and feet do not jam in them easily. Fist cracks are too big to get a hand jam, but not big enough to get your arm into. Fist jams are just what they sound like—place your fist in the crack and squeeze. Since flesh is the only thing that is jamming—unlike finger and hand jams, wherein the bone structure is helping—fist jams are notoriously insecure. Your hand orientation is important. Try your palm in or out to see which gives a better jam. In case you have to make several fist jams in a row, palm in on the top one and palm out on the bottom one will allow you to make longer and hopefully more secure reaches. The lower jam makes a good anchor while you shuffle the upper jam higher in the crack. Fortunately, fist cracks rarely go on forever.

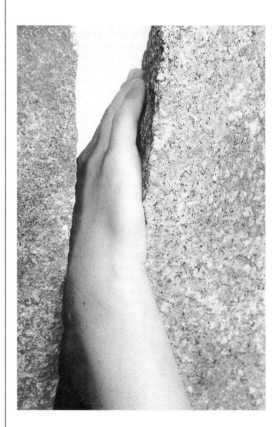

The thumb-down hand jam adds camming action.

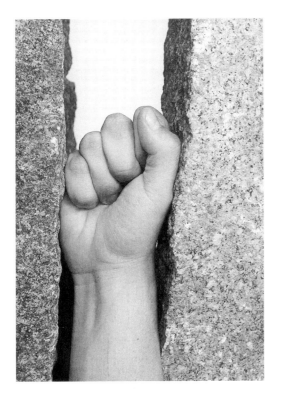

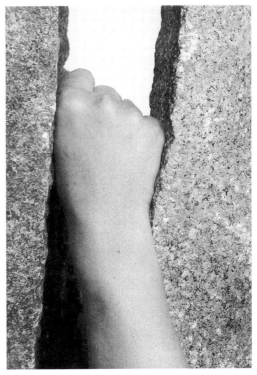

The fist jam—often insecure and painful. It's an acquired taste.

Another option for the fist jam.

Offwidth Cracks

Offwidth cracks are among the hardest to master. Long sections of offwidth climbing can be incredibly difficult and strenuous, and progress is often made millimeters at a time. Still, some aficionados will travel for days when they hear of the latest offwidth test piece. Science has yet to find a cure for this malady.

Offwidths range from just past fist width to those that will accept your body sideways. For narrow offwidths, a combination of fist jam and hand jam, called a hand stack, can make a jam with decent security. However, the next move is always a problem because both hands are used on the same hold. Foot stacks and knee jams can give a moment of pause while the hands are repositioned. When the crack is too wide for hand stacks, a host of other techniques come into play, some that allow you to stick in the crack and others, amazingly, that allow some upward progress.

"Arm bars" consist of sticking your entire arm into the crack and trying to oppose your palm, elbow, and shoulder against the sides. A

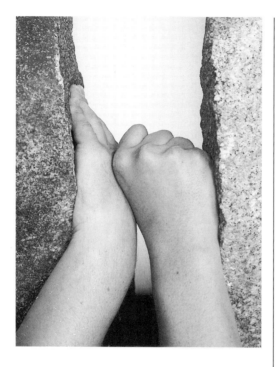

The hand-stack may be the only hold available on an offwidth crack; you'll wish you had a third hand.

little wider, and you can get a "chicken wing," wherein the entire arm is stuffed in and then the arm bent back out toward the front. This can actually give a very secure jam.

A hard thing about offwidths is often what to do with your "other" arm—the one not buried in the slot. Palming inside the crack at waist level, pushing against the outside edge of the crack, using face holds outside the crack, and other such contortions will often give you a chance to reposition your foot stack and chicken wing, and wiggle upward. Which side of your body you put in an offwidth crack is often key to success. There is no real rule here. You will figure it out soon enough.

Chimney Cracks

Chimneys range from the "squeeze" type, wherein your whole body can just barely fit in, to huge cracks that take a gymnast's flexibility to stem across. Chimneys are often not very difficult, and allow for fast and frequently really fun climbing. However, if there are no smaller cracks inside to get gear into, they can be impossible to protect. Chimneys are climbed by counter pressure: back against one wall, and hands and knees or feet against the other. In any chimney, the presence of holds inside the crack helps make progress easier.

In narrow chimneys, the back and feet will be against one wall and hands and knees against the other. Progress is made by holding your weight alternately with one set of counter-pressure holds while you move the other: Back and hands hold while feet and knees shuffle up, and then they hold while the back and hands scoot upward.

Wider chimneys allow you to put your back and hands against one wall and your feet against the other. The feet walk up the wall while the hands hold momentarily as the back is repositioned. In really wide chimneys, you have to stem across, with one hand and foot on one wall and the other pair on the other.

THE LOW-DOWN ON FOOT SMEARS

Using your feet in the gym is usually as simple as picking a foothold and pushing off it. Indoors, nearly every foothold is a positive edge. Outdoors, the situation is much different. While there are lots of edges on many climbs, there are also many climbs without any discernible footholds at all. Friction slabs, smooth-walled corners, and many low-angle face climbs require footwork that relies on smearing ability and not edging.

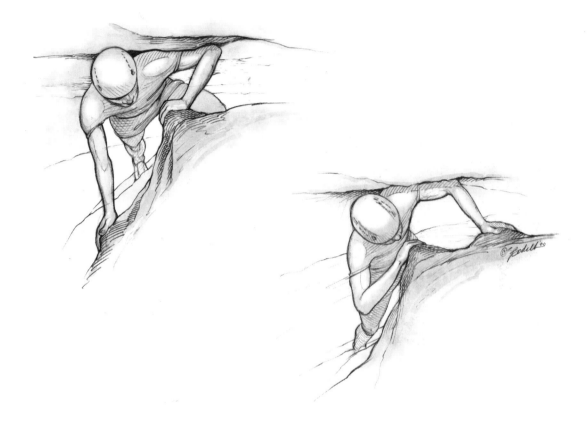

Two techniques for off-width cracks: the arm bar and the chicken wing

Smearing sounds simple: Just paste the bottom of your shoe on the rock, keep the force pushing in toward the rock as much as possible, and step up. If only it were that simple. Smearing can be very secure, and it can be incredibly tenuous. Many a talented gym climber has had his or her eyes opened on a runout section of 5.8 smearing. Here are a few tips:

■ Keep the bottom of your shoes really clean. Brush loose dirt off them, wet the sole, and scrub with the palm of your hand until it squeaks.

■ Keep the force straight in. The more perpendicular the line of force is to the rock, the better the smear will stick; keep your heel low.

■ Look for any irregularity. Even the merest divot or scoop can improve things dramatically.

■ Shift your weight smoothly and slowly. Hurried or jumpy movements will cause your foot to skid off.

■ Relax. Nothing makes a bad smear worse than "sewing machine legs," so go slow, breathe, and try not to let anxiety translate to a shaky leg.

TRADITIONAL LEADING

The leader standing at the base of a long free climb without a bolt in sight is facing one of the most exhilarating challenges in climbing. Making moves, keeping a cool head, searching for protection placements, routefinding, deciding when to stop, building a great belay anchor, and belaying up the rest of the party all take tremendous energy, ingenuity, and good judgment. The rewards are a great sense of accomplishment and hopefully a beautiful view. The three keys to safely leading a traditional pitch are:

Protect the moves. Place protection as frequently as necessary to protect you while you make difficult moves. Whether at an obvious crux move or just a place where you are not sure what is coming next, place good protection before you continue. On a traverse, protect the moves for your partner by placing protection frequently and especially just after any difficult move; if you make the move protected from behind you and then run it out on easy ground, imagine what your partner will be faced with. He or she will have to remove the protection that protected you, and then make the hard move with the potential of a very dangerous swing.

Protect the pitch. Be sure to keep your rope running in as straight a line as possible; unlike a sport route, where the bolts are usually lined up, a trad route may have protection spaced widely apart laterally. Put only a short quick-draw on each piece, and a fall may "zipper" your pieces. Place long slings when you go around corners or through overhangs, to minimize rope drag and the possibility of the rope running over a sharp edge. Quickdraws are not that useful on trad routes; carry lots of 24-inch slings and use them liberally. Make it your goal to lead the pitch quickly and efficiently; do not over- or underprotect it, and keep it safe for your second.

Protect the party. Build absolutely bombproof belay anchors and choose the best belay method for each situation. Belay in the right place—be *timely;* shorter pitches that maximize communication are often better than long ones on which it is difficult for the climbers to hear and see each other. If you get to a comfortable ledge with good anchor potential, stop and belay—running it out to the end of the rope and then fishing around for an anchor often wastes time and puts the party in awkward places to belay.

If you always place good protection for yourself and your partner, arrange the string of protection to minimize drag and the risk of pieces pulling out or doing damage to the rope, and build and properly use a great belay, then you will always climb as safely as possible. Do this over and over again on a multipitch climb, and you have succeeded in "bringing the ground up with you," and you can climb confidently and boldly.

GETTING STARTED

The start of a traditional lead begins with organizing the equipment. The rope should be stacked, helmets and harnesses put on (check those buckles!), and the rack selected and organized. Each climber ties into one end of the rope—the leader always climbs off the top end—a bottom anchor is built, and the belayer and climber go through the **CATCH** checklist to be sure the belay is ready (see the Belaying Outdoors section of chapter 2, Sport Climbing Outdoors, for a description of the **CATCH** principles). The belayer should be sure he or

Use slings to keep the rope running in a straight line or risk "zippering" the pitch.

she has enough equipment to escape the belay (in case of an emergency, the belayer should have extra carabiners and slings—see chapter 4, Retreat and an Introduction to Self-Rescue, for more information). Both climbers should agree on the signals that will be used to communicate, and then it is time to get going.

PLACING PROTECTION

As soon as the leader leaves the ground, he or she should be thinking about placing protection. The most dangerous point in a traditional lead is often the first few feet. If you do not place protection quickly, you risk falling and hitting the ground. It is also important that the first piece placed be multidirectional—able to hold a load in more than one direction. The first piece anchors the pitch. It provides the belayer with the correct point of alignment, and keeps each subsequent piece of protection from pulling out. The first piece of protection is thus often required to hold an outward, not just a downward, force. It must be bombproof. Many climbers set their first piece of protection before they leave the ground to ensure that the pitch will be anchored.

How often the leader places protection depends on many things, including how comfortable he or she is at the difficulty rating (a 5.12 climber on a 5.4 route will probably run a pitch out more than a 5.4 climber at his or her limit), the availability of good protection (remember those R and X ratings of seriousness), and how strenuous the climbing is (it may be easier to spread the pieces out a bit than to try to hang on every few feet on an overhanging wall). There is no rule: The leader should place as much protection as he or she

A multidirectional first piece of protection on a lead—a sign of a safe leader.

feels is necessary to provide an adequate level of safety.

When the leader stops to place protection, the first thing he or she should do is get as stable as possible—the leader is going to have to let go with at least one hand, after all. By working on body position, it is often possible to get stable in a spot that at first feels like it would be impossible to drop either hand. Once stable, examine the available cracks and pick the best spot for either a nut or a cam. If the choice is to be a nut, the leader can often get the right piece right away if he or she keeps a small range of nuts on one carabiner (a set of stoppers can be split into three or four mini-sets, each stored on one carabiner). By picking the carabiner with the right set of nuts on it, it is usually possible to find the right nut without going back to the rack for another try. Cams have a wider range than nuts, so they can usually be grabbed on the first try, even if racked singly. Efficiency is key—nothing is a bigger strength drain than fiddling endlessly trying to get the right nut by hanging from one hand on tiny holds. Practicing on the ground will help your efficiency on the cliff.

At each protection point, the leader must decide in what direction the piece is likely to be pulled in a fall; that helps determine the piece's correct orientation. It is sometimes necessary to set a second piece in opposition to the first to help ensure the primary piece will stay in its strongest alignment. A word of caution regarding cams: It is common for novices to place cams in a vertical crack with the shaft out of alignment with the fall line. The cam's shaft must be tipped down the crack—not sticking straight out. If a cam is placed with the shaft sticking straight out, it will likely rotate downward in a fall and may be dislodged.

With rare exceptions, every piece of protection will get some kind of sling extension. If the climb is straight up, quickdraws may be appropriate, but be aware that quickdraws can easily be levered upward as the leader passes and may dislodge the protection. Use longer slings to minimize rope drag and protect the rope from running over sharp edges.

Two nuts pulling in opposition to each other can make a very secure single-point anchor. A great method for connecting them is to clip a sling into one of them, run it through the second, and then back through the second one again. This creates a locking girth hitch around the second carabiner that locks in place, helping to maintain the strongest possible orientation for the nuts.

Two opposed nuts in a horizontal crack held in tension with the locking girth hitch.

This cam in a vertical crack is not properly aligned with the downward fall line. It will rotate when loaded and may fail—always place cams with their shafts aligned with the direction of anticipated force.

When using a rigid-stemmed cam in a horizontal crack, leverage will be reduced if you clip to it using a piece of cord tied through one of the holes further up the stem.

It has been mentioned before but bears repeating: Protect traverses. Even if the climbing is easy, place protection frequently on traverses; your second will appreciate it.

BELAYING THE SECOND

When the leader reaches the end of the pitch, he or she must build a belay anchor. The belay can take any form, from a tree or boulder to an anchor built entirely with gear or to even a combination of types (for example, a small tree and two nuts). After the belay has been made and the leader is off belay, it is time to decide how to belay the second. There are four basic options:

- belaying off the harness
- belaying directly off the anchor—including from a remote master point
- redirecting the belay off the anchor
- belaying off an extended master point

Off the Harness

This is by far the most common method for the leader to belay the second, though it is rarely the best choice. Belaying off the harness feels natural and it is straightforward, but it has drawbacks.

It places all the weight of the climber on the belayer's waist, and if he or she is not aligned and tight with the anchor, the belayer can be pulled out of position and lose control. If the second falls a lot and hangs around, shaking out to try the crux move repeatedly, the belayer will find it uncomfortable. Also, in an emergency it is harder to escape the belay if the belayer is belaying off the harness. Belaying off the harness is most appropriate when:

- the climb is low-angled or easily within the ability of the climber, and the belayer does not expect to hold the climber for long periods of time
- the anchor is situated so that it is easy for the belayer to be aligned and tight to the anchor

The top belay off the harness, a popular method yet rarely the best choice. The belayer should be aligned and tight to the anchor.

Belaying directly off the anchor is simple, secure, and convenient. The anchor must be bombproof and the proper device used—a Gri Gri or Munter hitch is best; plates and tubes are rarely applicable because they cannot be locked up readily.

Directly Off the Anchor

This method of the leader belaying the second is becoming increasingly popular, and rightfully so. The belay device is connected directly to the master point of the belay anchor and is not attached to the belayer at all. Belaying off the anchor has been standard practice for professional guides for many years, and is

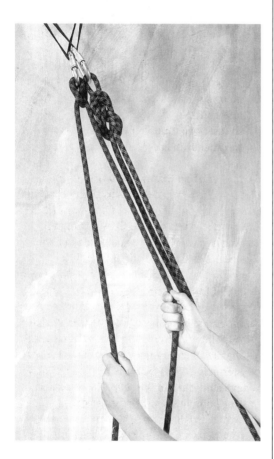

Using a Munter hitch off the anchor allows the belayer to belay from a remote position. This often allows him or her to see the climber more easily while still giving a belay all the way to the anchor.

catching on with recreational climbers as well. It is appropriate in many situations and has several distinct advantages:

- It is easy for the belayer to hold the climber—the anchor does all the work.
- The belay is automatically aligned and tight.
- It works very effectively with a Munter hitch or Petzl Gri Gri (it takes a lot of belaying strain off the belayer's shoulders).
- It can be operated remotely with a Munter hitch (for example, the pitch ends on a long, low-angled slab and the climber cannot be seen from the anchor; the belayer ties in long enough to belay from the edge of the slab and runs the rope through a Munter hitch on the anchor—he or she can see the climber and the climber is protected all the way to the belay).
- The force on the anchor is minimal—just the climber's body weight; with all other methods, the weight on the anchor is at least double body weight.
- In case of an emergency, escaping the belay can be done in a matter of seconds, and it is very easy to rig a raising system off the anchor.

Belaying off the anchor does come with some caveats however:

- Initially it does not feel as natural as belaying off the harness, and takes getting used to.
- It requires a better understanding of belay devices and their limitations (belay plates and tubes are usually not appropriate to use directly off the anchor because they cannot be locked off readily by the belayer).

Redirecting the Belay Off the Anchor

This is another useful technique that can make belaying the second more comfortable. It is a combination of the harness belay and the anchor belay. The belay device is placed on the belayer's harness, and then the rope is run up through the anchor and back down to the climber. It is really nothing more than a slingshot belay, with the belayer at the anchor instead of on the ground. It has several advantages:

- Operating the belay device is simple and feels natural.
- The belayer holds less weight than if he or she belayed from the harness because of the friction through the anchor.
- The belay is automatically aligned and tight.
- It can be used remotely (as in the situation described in the Directly Off the Anchor

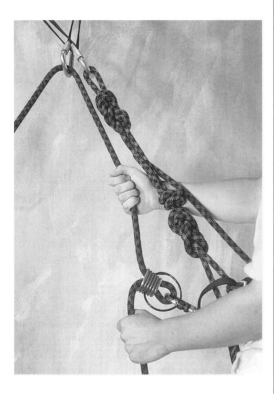

A redirected belay is just a slingshot belay operated close to the top anchor. The belayer should be prepared for an upward pull.

section above: the climber cannot be seen from the anchor, so the belayer ties in long enough to belay from the edge, clips the rope through a belay device on his or her harness, and runs the rope through a locking carabiner on the anchor—he or she can see the climber and the climber is protected all the way to the belay).

- It is easier to escape the belay than if belaying directly off the harness.

The following points should also be considered when considering the redirected belay:

- In order to be effective, the belayer must be braced for a pull toward the anchor—if not, he or she can be pulled out of position and lose control.
- At least two times body weight is applied to the anchor in case of a fall.

Off an Extended Master Point

This is a variation of the belay directly off the anchor. It is particularly useful in cases wherein the belayer needs to be well away from the anchor (in other words, to be able to see the climber) but the terrain does not call for protection all the way to the anchor (the anchor is 20 feet from the cliff edge on flat ground). The belayer ties in with enough slack to belay comfortably from the edge of the cliff. At that same point on the climber's strand of rope, he or she ties a figure eight on a bight loop as the master point. The climber is belayed through a device attached to this loop. The extended master point has several advantages:

- Any belay device can be used.
- The belay can be operated easily and smoothly because the device is right next to the belayer.
- Escaping the belay in an emergency is a snap.

As with the other systems described in this section, a couple of precautions apply:

The master point has been extended by tying a loop on the rope at the belayer's position. Belaying from an extended master point allows the belayer to be in the best position but keeps him or her free from the system—often a better option than belaying off the harness from the same point.

- It does not work well if the belayer is standing—the device will be at his or her feet. The method works best if the belayer is sitting, with the master point right next to him or her.
- When the climber falls, rope-stretch could pull the extended master point over the edge and it could stretch out of reach of the belayer. The master point should be tied slightly closer to the anchor than the belayer's

tie-in (but not so far behind that the belayer cannot lock off a plate or tube device).

Determining the most appropriate belay method is a matter of judgment and will be different for each belay. Practice the above methods on the ground before experimenting on the cliff, and always choose the method that you feel provides the highest degree of security.

SECONDING A PITCH

The second removes the bottom belay anchor and all the intermediate protection as he or she climbs the pitch. If the climb is just one pitch, or the first pitch of a multipitch route, the second can begin the job of dismantling the belay as soon as the leader is tied in to the top anchor and shouts down, "Off belay." If the second is already up a pitch, then he or she must wait for the leader to pull up all the slack and put him or her on belay before beginning to break down the anchor.

The second needs to be organized, especially on a long multipitch route. He or she must remove the gear and store it in a logical fashion. Nothing slows a climb down more than having the second arrive at the belay with nuts and slings all clipped to each other and draped haphazardly all over the place.

Removing the belay is usually straightforward because the second is on a good stance. If the belay is a hanging stance, the second may have to climb up a move or two and get established on the climb while removing the anchor; in extreme situations, he or she may need to hang on the rope while working. Here are a few pointers for removing and racking gear while seconding:

1. When you get to a piece of protection,

KEY TRANSITION EXERCISE: LEARNING THE VITAL SKILLS FOR CLIMBING OUTSIDE
Learning the Various Top-Belay Options and Their Applications

THE CHALLENGE

Safely belaying a climber from above is not easy. Many variables can make choosing a safe method perplexing. The best choice is not always obvious and climbers are often put at unnecessary risk.

THE DIFFERENCE BETWEEN BELAYING FROM ABOVE INDOORS AND OUTDOORS

Indoors: You do not belay from above indoors. Whether you are performing a lead belay or using a top-rope, the belayer always stands on the ground and belays off the harness. The direction of force is always upward and always obvious.
Outdoors: Belaying from above is common outdoors. On some single-pitch routes and on all multipitch routes, the belayer is above the climber when he or she is seconding a pitch. The anchors are not always in a convenient place, and the direction of force is not always obvious.

THE GOAL

Master the basic top-belay options by practicing each of the basic systems, and develop an understanding of their applications so that the best choice will be made in each situation.

THE EQUIPMENT

    2 climbing harnesses
    3 locking carabiners
    1 two-point anchor
    1 rope
    1 belay/rappel device
    1–3 24-inch slings (for use on a single-point anchor, such as a tree)

THE SETUP

The standard two-point anchor setup or, even easier, a single-point anchor consisting of a sling girth-hitched around a tree or post can be used (see How to Use This Book in the Introduction).

The Top-Belay Options Exercise

This exercise consists of learning about and practicing the five most common top-belay options:

- off the harness
- off the anchor
- off a remote anchor
- redirected through the anchor
- off an extended master point

Off the Harness

1. Set up the standard two-point anchor.
2. Have the belayer and climber each tie in to an end of rope.
3. Have the belayer tie a figure eight on a bight and clip it in to the anchor as his or her tie-in.
4. Go through the **CATCH** checklist.
5. Practice taking rope in, feeding rope out, and holding falls while belaying off the harness.
6. Use several different devices.
7. Switch places and repeat steps 3 through 6.

Off the Anchor

1. Repeat steps 1 through 3 in the Off the Harness option above.
2. Attach either a Munter hitch or Petzl Gri Gri to the anchor's master point.
3. Put the climber on belay and practice feeding rope out, taking rope in, and holding falls.
4. Repeat with other devices, including plates and tubes, and note the serious limitation of these devices when belaying off the anchor.
5. Switch rope ends and repeat steps 3 through 6.

Off a Remote Anchor

1. Repeat steps 1 and 2 in the Off the Harness option above.
2. Have the belayer tie a figure eight on a bight and clip it in to the anchor as his or her tie-in with at least 10 feet of slack between him or herself and the anchor.
3. Attach a Munter hitch to the anchor's master point.
4. Put the climber on belay and practice feeding rope out, taking rope in, and holding falls.
5. Repeat with the Petzl Gri Gri.
   Note: Slack can be fed out slowly through an unweighted Gri Gri, but under a load the belayer will have to move up toward the anchor and use the Gri Gri's release lever to feed out slack.
6. Experiment with plates and tubes just to drive home the point that they should never be used off a remote anchor.
7. Switch rope ends and repeat steps 2 through 6.

Redirecting a Belay

1. Repeat steps 1 through 3 in the Off the Harness option above.
2. Attach any device to the belayer's harness.
3. Clip the climber's rope through the master point of the anchor with a locking carabiner.
4. Put the climber on belay and practice feeding rope out, taking rope in, and holding falls.
5. Repeat with other devices.
6. Switch rope ends and repeat steps 3 through 5.

Off an Extended Master Point
1. Repeat steps 1 and 2 in the Off the Harness option above.
2. Have the belayer tie a figure eight on a bight and clip it in to the anchor as his or her tie-in—at least 6 feet from the anchor.
3. Tie a figure eight on a bight loop on the climber's end of the rope the same distance from the belay anchor as the belayer's tie is; attach any belay device to it and put the climber on belay.
4. Practice feeding rope out, taking rope in, and holding falls.
5. Repeat with other devices and take note of how effectively they belay; make changes in the position of the master point loop as necessary.
6. Switch rope ends and repeat steps 2 through 5.

first try to establish a stable stance—after all, the leader figured out a way to stand there comfortably enough to put the piece in.

2. After you are as stable as you can be, look at the piece before you take it out: Which way did it go in? Should it be pulled up? Out and up? Twisted and then tugged upward? You get the picture.

3. Keep pieces clipped to the rope while you work to get them out. If the piece is on a quickdraw, after it is out of the rock, clip the carabiner that is attached to the nut to the gear sling, then unclip the other carabiner from the rope and let it dangle—this ensures that you will not drop the nut while you work to get it out and that once it is out it does not hang down too far (as it would if you clipped the other carabiner to the gear sling). If the piece is on a long sling, take the piece out, put the sling over your head and shoulder, then unclip the sling from the rope.

4. If a nut was set well by the leader, it may take a tap from the nut tool to loosen it (keep the nut tool clipped to something while you poke at the nut).

5. If the piece is a cam, be careful to grab it carefully and retract the cams at the same time you push on the stem—if you grab it blindly or accidentally push it in, it may be stuck forever.

6. Put each piece where it belongs, and keep like things together as you go: slings with slings, nuts with nuts, cams with cams, et cetera.

7. When storing extra-long slings or cordelettes, wrap them up into a small package first and then store them—do not just let them drape all over you.

8. If a placement is in a particularly difficult place to work—in the middle of a crux sequence, for instance—quickly analyze it, pop it out, and let it slide down and hang on the rope by your tie-in knot. You can store it when you get to a good stance.

When you get to the belay, tie a figure eight loop in the rope to form a tether, and clip into the anchor with a locking carabiner or two carabiners reversed and opposed, then prepare to make the transition to the next step on the climb.

TRANSITIONS

A key to safe climbing is the ability to efficiently and effectively change from one climbing system to another; for example, from one pitch to the next, or from climbing to rappelling. The steps involved in these "transitions" depend on the activity and can be complex. Planning and organization are the keys. Below are the fundamental transitions:

- from climbing to descent by walking off
- from climbing to descent by lowering
- from climbing to descent by rappelling on single-pitch climbs
- from climbing one pitch to the next on multipitch climbs
- from climbing to descent by lowering or rappelling on multipitch climbs (this transition is covered in chapter 4, Retreat and an Introduction to Self-Rescue)

FROM CLIMBING TO DESCENT BY WALKING OFF

This is the simplest of all transitions, but precautions should be taken nonetheless. When the second arrives at the top, the simplest thing is for him or her to stay on belay and walk away from the cliff until secure. If the initial part of the walk-off is potentially dangerous, then the second should establish a quick anchor (for example, a braced stance, walk the rope around a tree, et cetera) and provide a quick belay for the leader as he or she dismantles the belay and walks off.

FROM CLIMBING TO DESCENT BY LOWERING

On a single-pitch climb with fixed anchors, if the plan is for the leader to belay from above

Clipping in to the anchor with a sling girth-hitched to your harness helps increase efficiency when making transitions (for example, going from climbing to rappelling).

and for both climbers to lower from the anchors after the climb, the transition sequence is this:

1. When the leader arrives at the belay, he or she should clip into it with a sling girth-hitched to the harness instead of with a figure eight leash on the rope—

this will expedite the leader's transition to lowering later.

2. When the second arrives, he or she can be immediately lowered to the ground. The gear that the second collected can either be transferred to the leader before the lower begins, or the second can take it down.

3. After the second arrives on the ground and is off belay, he or she pulls all the rope down and puts the leader on belay.

4. The leader pulls up 5 feet or so of slack, ties an overhand loop, and clips it to the harness or the anchor to store it. This ensures that the leader will not drop the rope during the transition.

5. The leader now unties the rope from the harness, (remember, he or she is clipped to the anchor with a sling), threads it through the anchor's lowering/rappel ring, reties into the harness, and unties the overhand loop.

6. The leader shouts "Take" to the belayer; the belayer takes in all the slack and locks off the belay.

7. The leader unclips his or her sling leash, stores it, and shouts "Ready to lower."

8. The belayer lowers the leader to the ground.

FROM CLIMBING TO DESCENT BY RAPPELLING ON SINGLE-PITCH CLIMBS

This is another common transition that is made smoother and safer by planning and organization. We look at this transition in two ways: In the first, the first climber to rappel requires an overhead belay (because he or she is unfamiliar or uncomfortable with an autoblock self-belay), and in the second, both climbers are competent with self-belays.

Below is the procedure when one rappeller needs an overhead belay; an alternative to this method is the prerigged rappel (see chapter 4, Retreat and an Introduction to Self-Rescue):

1. When the leader arrives at the belay, he or she clips into it with a sling girth-hitched to the harness instead of with a figure eight leash on the rope—this will expedite the transition to rappelling later.

2. When the second arrives, he or she clips into the anchor by tying a figure eight on a bight on the rope and clipping it to the anchor for a leash. The leader leaves the second on belay.

3. The second rope (trailed or carried in a pack by either climber) is uncoiled, one end is threaded through the anchor, the leader unties his or her lead rope, and the two ropes are tied together.

4. A figure eight on a bight loop is tied on the second climbing rope just below the knot joining the ropes, and clipped to the anchor to fix that rope.

5. The second rope becomes the rappel line; a knot is tied in the end of it and it is dropped.

6. The second attaches his or her rappel device to the rappel rope, unclips his or her leash, unties his or her figure eight on a bight, and rappels with a belay from above, on the original rope.

7. When the second is safely on the ground, the leader attaches his or her rappel device to both strands, establishes a backup belay (either an autoblock or a fireman's belay from below), unclips the figure eight on a bight knot on the rope, unclips his or her sling leash, and rappels.

Below is the procedure when both climbers are competent with self-belays:

1. When the leader arrives at the belay, he or she clips into it with a sling girth-hitched to the harness instead of with a figure eight leash on the rope—this will expedite the transition to rappelling later.

2. When the second arrives, he or she clips into the anchor with a sling girth-hitched to the harness.

3. Both climbers can now untie the rope from their harnesses and thread the rope through the anchor's lowering/rappel ring, tie the ends together in an over-hand knot, and pull it through to the middle mark.

   Note: Tie an overhand loop in the ropes and clip them to something while you work to ensure you won't lose them.

4. The first climber to rappel threads the rope through his or her rappel device, clips it to the sling girth-hitched to his or her harness with a locking carabiner, establishes the autoblock backup (for details on setting this up, see chapter 4, Retreat and an Introduction to Self-Rescue), unclips the sling from the anchor, and rappels.

5. The second climber can now repeat the process (a fireman's belay from below will eliminate the need for the autoblock backup for the second climber).

FROM CLIMBING ONE PITCH TO THE NEXT ON MULTIPITCH CLIMBS

Multipitch climbing is one of the joys of traditional climbing. If you can safely lead pitches and build and use belay anchors correctly, then the sky is the limit—you can climb routes as long as your abilities and dreams can take you.

On multipitch climbs, the smooth transition from one pitch to the next can mean the difference between completing a long climb before dark or climbing the last pitch by headlamp. The transition is greatly stream-lined by planning and organization:

■ Carry what you need—including extra equipment, clothing, food, and water, et cetera—but keep the packs free from superfluous stuff that would slow you down.

■ Be sure to keep the rack and equipment as organized as possible: The second should take extra care to store the gear from a pitch in a way that makes it fast and easy to transfer it back to the lead rack.

■ Make good rope management a priority; nothing slows a party down like untangling ropes at each belay.

■ Think before you clip things together; a lot of time can be wasted by clipping and unclipping things unnecessarily.

This is the basic sequence for the belay transition on a multipitch climb:

1. While the second is climbing, the leader either stacks the rope neatly on the ledge, lets it hang down out of the way (be careful that the rope cannot get hung up on things below the belay), or "butterflies" the rope across his or her leash.

2. When the second arrives, he or she clips into the anchor with a figure eight on a bight leash, making sure that the length will be correct for belaying the leader on the next pitch.

3. The second gives the gear back to the leader a piece at a time (even if the

"Butterflying" the rope back and forth across your rope tether is a good way to keep the rope organized when you are belaying from small stances.

second will lead the next pitch, it is easier to give the gear back to the original leader—it will be easy to transfer the completed rack back to the second). When transferring gear, do not hurry and do not get distracted; make eye contact and be certain that the leader has a firm grip on the gear before releasing it. Ask questions: "Got it?" "Yup, got it."

4. After the gear is transferred and organized, the leader of the next pitch should organize him or herself while the belayer restacks or rebutterflies the rope to put the leader's end on top (if you fail to do this, you will inevitably get the rope tangled).

5. The belayer then puts the leader on belay and things are ready to go.

6. Before the leader leaves the belay, he or she gets in the first piece of protection (this eliminates the possibility of a fall that must be caught directly by the belayer's harness). The best situation is one in which a bomber piece can be placed just above the belay anchor. If that cannot be done, then the leader should clip the master point of the belay as the first piece and then plan on getting the next piece as soon as possible.

7. Repeat the sequence until the top of the climb is reached.

CHAPTER 4

Retreat and an Introduction to Self-Rescue

"What goes up, must come down" is a familiar adage. It also begs the question for climbers: "If you go up, can you get down?" The ability to get out of an emergency by yourself using standard climbing equipment is vital for every climber who leaves the ground. Even something as fundamental as ascending a rope with prusik cords can mean, and has meant, the difference between life and death.

Years ago in New Hampshire, two young climbers were on the last pitch of a six-pitch route on Cannon Mountain. The leader had reached the top but the second was unable to negotiate the final strenuous (5.5) move 40 feet below. If the second had known how to ascend a rope using a prusik, he could have overcome the 5-foot obstacle and finished the easy climbing above. Instead his partner called for a rescue. More than 3 hours after the climber had been stuck, the Mountain Rescue Service arrived with twenty expert volunteers. The rescue was over in 5 minutes and everyone went home relieved. However, had it been a

different night, had they become stuck at dusk, if freezing rain and wind had set in, they may not have survived. And all because they did not know how to use a hitch that takes a few minutes to learn.

Self-rescue is a complex subject. Entire books have been devoted to the subject. What follows here are the fundamentals, the tools, and the techniques that can get you out of trouble most of the time. In cases of dire emergency, where there are life-threatening injuries or irreversible problems, these techniques may help, but a full-scale rescue may also be required.

Self-rescue should not be experimented with under stress. Practice every technique on the ground and be totally confident before you try it in real life. Self-rescue is interesting, the techniques are clever and often surprisingly quick and efficient, but what follows is serious stuff. These are not cute rope tricks to be pulled out of your pack when you want to impress someone. Learn how to climb safely, understand the basics of getting out of trouble, and use the right technique at the right time—and you should have a long and fulfilling climbing career.

EQUIPMENT

The first step to getting out of trouble is understanding that bad things happen to good climbers, and preparation is the key. Prevention is vital, but when you do everything right and things still go wrong, you need to have the right equipment and the right skills to rescue yourself.

The equipment to facilitate self-rescue is the same equipment that you would normally carry on a multipitch route. Nothing is specialized or exotic. However, in order to be effective, the tools for self-rescue should be carried by everyone in the party at all times. When the *Titanic* sunk, there were not enough lifeboats to hold all the crew and passengers.

In climbing, it does not do anyone any good if there is not enough basic rescue equipment to go around. What happens if the leader is the only one with the equipment, but the second needs a prusik to get past a move he or she cannot do? Every climber should carry the following minimum equipment at all times:
   three 24-inch slings
   one 24-inch loop made from 7 mm perlon
   four extra carabiners
   two locking carabiners, at least one of them
      large and pear-shaped
   one cordelette (a 10- to 16-foot loop of 7 mm
      or equivalent cord, tied with a double
      fisherman knot)
   one belay/rappel device
   two rappel rings

RAPPELLING

Rappelling is the single most important self-rescue technique to master. Getting out of a jam is often just a matter of rappelling down, and the safer and faster you can do it, the better. However, rappelling is also one of the most dangerous activities of all if the proper tools and techniques are not applied. In belayed climbing, the rope, the protection, the anchor, and the belayer all serve as a backup—if no one falls, then the entire system was superfluous. Rappelling, on the other hand, relies on the rope, anchor, and self-belay at all times. There is no room for error.

Phrases like "rappel anchor pulled out," "climber rappelled off the end of the rope," and "climber lost control of the rappel" are all too frequently written in the American Alpine Club's annual publication *Accidents in North American Mountaineering.* Master the skills in this chapter and apply them correctly, and you lessen your chances of your name appearing in that book.

The equipment for rappelling can be as simple as a locking carabiner and a rappel device. Figure eights or tube-style belay/rappel devices work best, though plates, carabiners alone, or even the Munter hitch can be used in a pinch. The three critical elements to safe rappelling are:

▪ The rappel anchor must be solid and secure.
▪ The rappeller must use proper technique to maintain control during the descent.
▪ There should be a system backup.

The Rappel Anchor

The fundamentals of anchoring are covered in chapter 2, Sport Climbing Outdoors, and chapter 3, Traditional (Rock) Climbing, but there are a few things to consider when an anchor will be used for a rappel. If the anchor is fixed (for example, two bolts with a chain and lap link or ring), then all you need to do is thread the rope and go. With all anchors, be absolutely certain that the rope will not rub against any potentially dangerous edges during the rappel—ropes under tension cut very easily!

If the anchor is one you have built yourself, it must be **SECURE** (see chapter 3, Traditional (Rock) Climbing). For rappelling, the anchor should ideally be situated high enough so the rappeller does not have to make an awkward transition over the cliff edge or off the ledge before he or she begins the descent. The ideal rappel anchor enables the person rappelling to assume the correct body position and put his or her weight on the rope before going over the edge. If this is not possible, a separate belay rope can be used to help ensure safety and maintain control while the rappeller is making the transition over the edge.

Trees are commonly used as rappel anchors. They are usually very strong and, if they are big enough, the anchor can be constructed high on their trunks, which makes the transition over the edge easier. However, trees—even big ones—should be treated carefully. If climbing ropes are frequently wrapped directly around the tree and then weighted, the resulting wear will damage the bark and, if done often enough, can even kill the tree. Pulling the rope around the tree can also damage the rope—heat builds up and can melt the sheath. In order to keep trees healthy (and thus extend their life as bombproof anchors), try to always do the following:

▪ Whenever possible, wrap the tree using a sling and carabiners to create your anchor.
▪ If the tree will be used frequently for rappelling, consider creating a semiper-

manent anchor with slings and rappel rings (semipermanent because the slings will need to be replaced occasionally).

■ If you must wrap the rope directly around the tree, pull the rope very slowly after the rappel to minimize friction damage to the bark or the rope.

It is common when rappelling multipitch routes to find rappel anchors consisting of multiple slings around trees or through fixed anchors such as pitons. Do not assume that just because there is a lot of webbing, the anchor is reliable. Check each individual anchor, and do not rappel until you are satisfied that it is strong enough. Be wary of the "American Triangle," which consists of a sling or slings tied through two anchors (pitons or bolts), forming a triangle. This configuration needlessly increases the stress on each anchor point.

Additionally, fixed sling anchors often are not equipped with rappel rings, meaning that parties before you might have wrapped their rope around the slings themselves. Check the slings for wear at the point where the ropes might have been rubbing on them. Frayed or melted slings should not be trusted. The best thing that you can do in situations like this is to cut away any slings that appear old or are damaged, replace them by tying new slings to each anchor separately, threading rappel rings into the loops tied into the ends of the slings at the master point. You now have created a safer anchor with less stress on the individual anchor points, and a durable master point to run the rope through.

Proper Technique

Proper rappelling technique can save your life. The correct equipment, body position, and rope handling will keep you in control—making every rappel just a simple slide down the rope. The ten commandments for safe rappelling technique are:

1. Keep all loose clothing, hair, slings, helmet straps, and all other equipment away from your rappel device: If anything gets caught, you may be trapped or lose control.

2. Keep your brake hand on the rope: If you let go, you could lose complete control of your descent.

3. Keep your brake hand on your hip, feeding rope out by relaxing your fingers: If your brake hand creeps up toward your rappel device, you may get pinched and let go.

4. Keep your upper body upright: Many beginners lean in, making it much harder to see where they are going and increasing the likelihood that clothing or hair will be trapped by the belay device.

5. Keep your toes on the rock and your heels low: This ensures that your body position will be correct and that your feet will not get too low—if they do, they may slip, sending you face first into the cliff.

6. Go slow and take short steps: Do not rappel the way they do on TV; "be all you can be" by not bouncing, bounding, or taking big, fast drops—walking down slowly will keep you in control and minimize the stress and wear on your equipment.

7. Watch where you are going: Look down, make decisions where to step; if you are caught by surprise by a ledge or overhang, you may lose control.

8. Stay in the fall line: Stray to the side, and you may swing dangerously if you lose your footing.

9. Be cautious on overhangs: Small overhangs are no problem—just step over them—but overhangs bigger than about 2 feet could cause you to smash your knuckles against the cliff as you swing under them, and you could let go; if you cannot step easily over the overhang, stop with your feet at the lip, lower yourself down until your hands are below the lip, and then gently step off—you will swing under the roof, the rope will contact the lip above your hands, and you should be able to maintain control.

10. On a multipitch rappel, stay on rappel until you are securely clipped to the next anchor: Do not decide to hang around without being clipped in—even on big ledges.

The System Backup

Use a solid anchor and proper technique, and you will probably never use a backup. But bad things can happen even when you are diligent: Hazards like falling rocks, bees, and lightning sometimes just happen. Many climbers, competent with building and assessing anchors and proficient in the techniques of rappelling, do not realize the risk they take by not backing up the system. Most rappelling accidents occur because the climbers break one of the ten commandments of rappelling technique, and are injured or killed because they have failed to establish a system backup. This is often because they do not understand the three simple backup methods, or they feel that backing up is unnecessary and too time consuming. Backing up the system is always easy—get in the habit of doing it.

The most fundamental backup is to tie a large knot, such as a figure eight on a bight, on the end of the rope or ropes. Do this on every rappel—unless you know absolutely that the ends of the rope are on the ground. If you do this, you will never run the risk of rappelling off the end of your rope. But you can still fall all the way to the end of the rope. The following three methods provide quick and secure ways to maximize safety during a rappel by stopping you immediately if you lose control. After reading this section, you will have no reason to rappel without a backup—ever!

The Fireman's Belay. This simple method can be used anytime there is a climber positioned at the bottom of the rope, either on the ground or at an anchor. The person below holds the rappel rope loosely while the rappeller is descending. If the rappeller loses control, the belayer can stop him or her immediately by pulling down on the rope—the belayer's hands take the place of the rappeller's brake hand. The belayer can hold the rappeller securely—with surprisingly little effort—until control is regained. The belayer then loosens his or her grip on the rope and the rappeller continues to descend. This is a very quick method that requires nothing more than a strong grip and good attention on the part of the belayer.

The Separate Belay-Rope Belay. This method can be used when there is no one below to provide a fireman's belay, but there is a belayer and extra rope available at the rappel anchor. It is especially useful when the transition over the edge is difficult or when the person rappelling is a novice, because it provides an extra feeling of security. Using whatever top belay method will work best, simply tie a separate rope to the rappeller and

Using a separate belay rope provides a safe backup for a rappel, especially when the rappeller is a novice or the transition over the edge is difficult.

give a belay during the descent. If the rappeller loses control or there is some emergency (hair caught in the rappel device), the belayer can stop him or her immediately.

The Autoblock Belay. If a separate belay rope is not available or a fireman's belay is not possible (for example, rappelling first on a multipitch route when both ropes are being used), then the rappeller can set up an "autoblock" backup. If more climbers knew about and used this technique, the number of rappelling accidents could be reduced dramatically. The only extra pieces of

equipment needed are a locking carabiner, a 16- to 24-inch 6–7 mm prusik loop, and a 24-inch sling (every climber should have these on hand—see the Equipment section at the beginning of this chapter). The steps for the autoblock backup are as follows:

1. Girth-hitch the sling to the harness.
2. Attach the rappel device to the rope and clip it to the sling with a locking carabiner.
3. Clip the second locking carabiner to the harness.
4. Clip the prusik loop to the second

Putting an autoblock hitch on the rope below the rappel device gives the rappeller a quick and secure self-belay.

carabiner, position the knot farthest away from the carabiner, wrap the loop around the rope (both strands) below the rappel device four to six times (more wraps yield more holding power), and then clip the loop back into the second carabiner—this forms the autoblock. (A standard 24-inch sling can also be used to form the autoblock, though it may take more wraps than cord does to hold securely.)

Once the system is in place, the rappel proceeds as usual, with two minor differences: The rappel device is now about 2 feet away from the harness, which feels weird at first (you will get used to it), and your brake hand now has to hold something during the rappel. Hold the autoblock loosely in your brake hand during the rappel. Now, if you let go of your brake hand accidentally (if it is hit by a falling rock) or need to use both hands to do something such as unclip a quickdraw, the autoblock will clamp down on the rope and hold you in place. To release the autoblock, simply pull it downward. It releases easily because it is only asked to take the place of your brake hand, and thus only has to hold a small amount of weight—the same amount you hold with your brake hand to stop yourself. In another method that uses a prusik hitch attached above the rappel device, the sling must hold all the climber's weight. This causes it to clamp very tightly to the rope, which makes it difficult to release. The autoblock is much easier to use.

STANDARD MULTIPITCH RAPPELLING

To rappel effectively pitch after pitch, climbers need to be able to make their transition at each belay station as quickly and as safely as possible. These days, with so many routes equipped with fixed anchors, many people are rappelling routes they used to walk off from. With the right procedures, the time spent at each belay can be kept to a minimum—just a couple of minutes in most cases. The ability to efficiently rappel pitch after pitch may save your life—in the case of an approaching thunderstorm—or at least make life more comfortable by getting you to the ground while it is still light. For a party of two climbers who are equally proficient, rappelling from anchor to anchor, each equipped with rappel rings, the following system works very well:

1. Each climber clips to the first anchor with a sling girth-hitched to the harness and a locking carabiner.
2. One climber unties the climbing rope from the harness while the second climber prepares the extra rope for the rappel by uncoiling and stacking it (the second climber stays tied into his or her end of the climbing rope at this time—if both ends are untied at once, the rope can be accidentally dropped).
3. The first climber threads his or her end of the climbing rope through the anchor and ties it to the bottom end of the extra rope.
4. The first climber then prepares to rappel by attaching his or her device to the rope, clipping it to his or her anchor sling with a locking carabiner, and clipping in his or her autoblock backup; at the same time, the second climber unties the rope tied to his or her harness, ties figure eight knots in the bottom end of each rope—so that no one can rappel off the end of the rope—and then throws both ropes off.
5. The first climber unclips from the anchor and rappels while the second climber attaches his or her autoblock backup to the rappel ropes (the second cannot clip his or her device in yet because the rope is taut).
6. When the first climber arrives at the next anchor, he or she clips the free locking carabiner on the rappel sling into the anchor, removes his or her device and backup, and shouts "Off rappel!"
7. The second climber pulls up slack, attaches his or her device, unclips from

the anchor, yells "On rappel," and descends.

8. When the second climber arrives at the belay, he or she clips in with his or her locking carabiner and removes his or her device and backup from the rope; while the second is doing this, the first climber pulls up the rope ends, unties the backup knots, feeds the slack from the correct strand through the anchor ring (the correct strand is always the strand that is on the knot side of the anchor—you cannot pull a knot through an anchor no matter how strong you are), and ties another backup knot in it.
9. The second climber now pulls the free strand through the top anchor while the first climber feeds it through the current anchor; when the knot attaching the two ropes is reached, and sometimes before, the second rope will fall from the top anchor; when it does, the second climber should try to control it, grab it near the end, and tie a knot in the end before tossing it off for the next rappel.
10. Repeat steps 4 through 9 for each pitch.

PRERIGGED RAPPELS

If two climbers need to rappel, whether on a single or multipitch route, and one of them is not able to rig his or her own rappels, then prerigging is a viable option.

1. Both climbers are attached to the anchor with slings girth-hitched to their harnesses.
2. The rope is threaded through the anchor as in the other systems.
3. The more experienced climber attaches his or her rappel device and autoblock backup as usual.
4. The other climber's rappel is set up for him or her by the more experienced

The prerigged rappel: the second rappeller cannot slide down the rope while the first climber is descending because the rope is tight. The first climber down can give the second rappeller a fireman's belay. During the first rappel the second climber should also be clipped to the anchor with a sling girth-hitched to the harness (not shown).

climber: A second sling is girth-hitched to the novice climber's harness and attached with a locking carabiner to a rappel device that is prerigged on the rappel rope above the first climber's device.

5. The experienced climber weights the rappel and engages his or her autoblock backup to hold him or herself in place.

The other climber is still clipped to the anchor and ready to rappel.

6. The experienced climber tells the other climber that he or she will be given a fireman's belay and can rappel as soon as he or she hears "on belay." The experienced climber now rappels to the next anchor and clips in with a sling.

7. The experienced climber slackens the rappel rope and yells "on belay, rappel when ready" and immediately begins giving the other climber a fireman's belay.

8. The other climber unclips his or her sling tie-in and begins rappelling. When the other climber reaches the belay, he or she clips into it with his or her anchor sling and goes off belay.

9. Both climbers now remove their belay devices, pull and thread the ropes through the new anchor and repeat steps 3 through 10 until they reach the ground.

RAPPELLING FROM A SPIDER

In a situation in which one climber is incapacitated and cannot rappel by him or herself (for example, if he or she has a broken arm), then both climbers can descend together using a simple spider. The spider rappel is only an emergency technique and should never be used when any simpler rappel method is adequate. For this example we assume one climber has a minor injury that leaves him or her ambulatory but unable to rappel unassisted.

1. Both climbers are attached to the anchor with slings girth-hitched to their harnesses.

2. The rope is threaded through the anchor as in the other systems.

3. The healthy climber takes a cordelette and ties a figure eight on a bight loop in it off-center so that two loops are formed,

The spider rappel allows two people to descend at the same time with the more able person controlling the rappel and backed up with an autoblock. This technique should be reserved for emergencies when one person is incapable of rappelling on his or her own. (A loop has been tied in the long end of the cordelette to shorten it.)

one about twice the size of the other—this forms the spider.

4. The figure eight on a bight loop is clipped to a rappel device attached to the rope; the healthy climber clips the short loop of the spider to his or her harness with a locking carabiner and establishes his or her autoblock backup as usual.

5. The longer loop on the spider is clipped to the injured climber's harness with a locking carabiner.

6. The healthy climber unclips his or her anchor sling, stores it, weights the rappel system, and allows the autoblock to hold them in position.

7. The injured climber's anchor sling is unclipped from the anchor and the healthy climber assists the injured climber down until he or she is hanging off the long loop in the spider (the healthy climber can use the injured climber's anchor as a hand line to help lower them to position); the injured climber's anchor sling is stored once they are hanging on the spider.

8. Both climbers are now "on rappel," each hanging from one loop of the spider (the disparity in the size of the loops separates the climbers vertically, helping to keep them from banging into each other on the way down), with the healthy climber controlling the rate of descent and backing up the system with his or her autoblock (extra wraps are advised on the autoblock because it will be holding twice the weight).

9. When the next anchor is reached, both climbers clip in with their anchor slings (on a big ledge where they both can stand, they can clip into the anchor at the figure eight loop on the spider—but the spider must be able to be slackened during the station transfer).

10. The healthy climber pulls and threads the ropes, reattaches the rappel device and the spider to the rope, and then repeats steps 6 through 10.

KEY TRANSITION EXERCISE: LEARNING THE VITAL SKILLS FOR CLIMBING OUTSIDE
Learning and Mastering Safe Rappelling Methods

THE CHALLENGE

Rappelling is a fundamental yet potentially dangerous skill. Unlike in climbing, wherein the system is only stressed when the climber falls, in rappelling the system is always stressed. Recreational climbers often fail to establish a backup for their rappels.

THE DIFFERENCE BETWEEN RAPPELLING INDOORS AND RAPPELLING OUTDOORS

Indoors: You do not rappel indoors.
Outdoors: Rappelling is a common and sometimes necessary skill that must be mastered to be done safely.

THE GOAL

Learn the fundamental rappel methods, including backups and systems to be used in emergencies.

THE EQUIPMENT

    1 two-point anchor
    2 24-inch slings
    4 locking carabiners
    1 rappel device
    1 cordelette

THE SETUP

The standard two-point anchor setup can be used to practice these exercises (see the How to Use This Book section of the Introduction).

The Rappel Exercise

All rappels should be belayed. There are three basic belay methods for protecting a rappel, and there is no good reason to rappel without a backup. Each method is simple and straightforward: belaying the rappeller on a separate rope tied to his or her harness (not described here), establishing an autoblock backup, or giving a fireman's belay from below, using a prerigged rappel. Practice these methods so that you will always be prepared to give a simple and safe belay.

    The spider rappel is for emergency use only. If you are fortunate, you will never have to use this method in a real climbing situation. It is not a party trick to be performed to show off. This technique places greater stress on the system and on the climbers than the two basic rappelling methods discussed here. There is less margin for error. Use it only if your life depends on the increased speed or efficiency.

These three rappel systems will cover just about any situation a climber will encounter. Every system has a belay backup. Make a promise to yourself right now never to rappel without a belay again! (In addition, make a practice of always tying your ropes together in a knot before tossing them down the cliff, to ensure that you can never rappel off the end of your rope.) This exercise demonstrates three systems:

- rappelling with an autoblock backup
- prerigging a rappel (and using a fireman's belay)
- emergency rappelling via the spider rappel

Rappelling with an Autoblock Backup

This rappel backup does not require a separate rope or belayer. It allows anyone to rappel with a belay—there is no excuse!

1. Pass the rope through the lap link on the standard anchor and run 20 or 30 feet through it.
2. The rappeller doubles a standard 24-inch sling through the harness (through the sewn belay/rappel loop, or through both the lower and upper straps if the harness does not have a belay/rappel loop) and clips a locking carabiner through to the two loops.
3. Thread the double rope through a rappel device and clip it to the locking carabiner on the doubled sling; lock the carabiner.
4. Clip the second locking carabiner to the harness; clip the second sling into it.
5. Wrap the sling around the two strands of rope below the belay device four or five times, then clip that end back in to the carabiner; lock the carabiner.
6. Weight the system and allow the autoblock to grip the rope and hold the rappeller's weight.
7. Practice loading and unloading the autoblock and rappelling while holding the autoblock loosely in the brake hand.

Note: The autoblock is the easiest method to provide a self-belay while rappelling. It works so marvelously because it is only required to replace the rappeller's brake hand—it does not have to hold full body-weight. Because of this, the autoblock holds securely but is easy to release because it is under little tension.

Another commonly recommended backup is to place a prusik above the belay device. This is not as easy to operate because: (1) the prusik must be kept loose during the rappel by the guide hand, which is unnatural; (2) the prusik must hold full body-weight when activated, which makes it much harder to release; and (3) because the sling is clipped to the harness below the rappel device but attached to the rope above it, it tends to get in the way of the whole operation. Once a climber tries the autoblock, he or she will probably never go back to the prusik again.

Prerigging a Rappel

This method is best used when speed is essential or when those rappelling after the lead rappeller are inexperienced and would benefit from a fireman's belay.

1. Pass the rope through the lap link on the standard anchor and run 20 or 30 feet through it.
2. Girth-hitch a 24-inch sling through the harness of the rappeller who will rappel second, thread the double rope through a rappel device, and clip it to the sling with a locking carabiner; lock the carabiner.
3. The first rappeller now establishes his or her rappel below the second rappeller's device, including an autoblock backup.
4. The first rappeller weights the system and allows the autoblock to hold his or her weight.
5. The second rappeller is protected from slipping by the weight of the first rappeller (it is impossible to rappel on a tight rope); try getting the second rappeller's device to slip down the rope.
6. The first rappeller rappels to the ground and gives the second rappeller a fireman's belay.
7. Switch positions and repeat steps 2 through 6.

Emergency Rappelling via the Spider Rappel

This rappel method should be used exclusively when a member of the party is injured and incapacitated but ambulatory—someone who cannot rappel safely on his or her own but can stand, walk, and communicate (for example, a climber with a broken arm, dislocated shoulder, et cetera). It is strictly an emergency system. Do not use this if any simpler method will work.

1. Thread the rope through the lap link on the anchor and run 20 or 30 feet through it.
2. Take a cordelette, double it, and tie an overhand loop off-center so that two loops are created, one about twice as long as the other.
3. Thread the ropes through a rappel device and clip it to the overhand loop in the cordelette; lock the carabiner.
4. Attach the cordelette loops to each rappeller's harness with a locking carabiner: the longer loop to the incapacitated climber's harness, the shorter one to the healthy climber's harness.
5. The healthy rappeller establishes an autoblock below the rappel device.
6. Both climbers weight the system and the healthy rappeller controls the party's descent.
7. Switch positions and repeat steps 2 through 6.

LOWERING

Lowering is one of the simplest descent techniques. It is something most climbers have done a lot, especially in the gym or at sport climbing areas, and uses standard climbing equipment and belay techniques. The belayer controls the descent of his or her partner by feeding rope out in a controlled manner through the belay system. Lowers occur with either the belayer positioned below the climber, as in the sport lower, or above the climber, when lowering down to top-rope from above, for example. Though the anchoring and belay systems may vary, no lower should be done without being sure that:

- the belay device is properly attached to the climber's harness (or the anchor) and is threaded correctly
- there is no loose clothing or equipment that might get caught in the belay device
- the belayer has chosen a method, anchor, and position that ensure he or she will maintain control of the descent
- a backup has been established if deemed necessary
- if lowering through an anchor, the anchor is appropriate—never lower through webbing or dangerously worn fixed anchors (chains, lap links, and even bolt hangers designed for lowering can get dangerously worn—always back up a suspect anchor)
- the rope is long enough so that the climber can reach the ground or the next belay—if the belayer reaches the end of the rope before the climber is in a secure position, a real emergency situation may develop
- the belayer is tied in to the end of the rope—this closes the system and guarantees that the belayer will never let the end of the rope slip through the belay device (failing to take this simple precaution has caused many accidents)
- communication is clear—both the climber and belayer must be clear on when and how the lowering is going to occur and what is going to happen after the climber is down (at least one accident occurred when a climber leaned back on the rope expecting to be lowered and fell to the ground because the belayer—thinking the climber would rappel—had taken him or her off belay)

- the belayer and climber have a backup plan in case of emergency (imagine what would happen if a climber is lowered off the top of a big cliff, cannot climb back up, and neither the climber nor the belayer has sufficient knowledge or equipment to improvise a rescue?)

THE SPORT LOWER

This is the most straightforward of all lowers, and standard practice on sport climbs. The belayer is positioned on the ground and when the climber is done, the belayer locks off the belay device, the climber weights the system, and the belayer slowly lowers the climber down. Typically the belayer is lowering off his or her harness, and his or her weight helps anchor the system. It sounds simple and almost always is. But in addition to the precautions above, there are a couple of things to watch out for:

- The belayer should be anchored if he or she is significantly lighter than the climber.
- Twists in the rope can jam inside the belay device—the belayer should be capable of dealing with this without jeopardizing the climber's safety.
- Whenever rockfall is a risk, the belayer should wear a helmet—he or she may lose control and drop the climber if he or she is struck in the head while performing the lower.

THE TOP LOWER

Lowering from above is also quite simple, but the system dynamics are significantly different from the sport lower. In the sport lower, the belayer's weight usually counterbalances the weight of the climber—the system feels balanced and relaxed. In the traditional top lower, the belayer lowers from his or her harness and must hold the weight of the climber directly. This can complicate the system to the point of failure if the appropriate anchor, belayer position, and belay device are not chosen. The belayer will be able to maintain far better control of the top lower in most instances if he or she lowers directly from the anchor. But if the belayer decides to lower from his or her harness, he or she should take the following precautions:

■ The belayer should be in line and tight to his or her anchor so he or she will not be pulled out of position when the system is weighted.

■ The belay device must be attached to the belayer by a keeper cord (accidents have occurred when unsecured belay plates slipped down the rope away from the belay—most devices come with keeper cords; use them).

■ The belayer must be absolutely sure that he or she can hold and control the weight of the climber until the lower is complete.

Working directly from an anchor is slowly becoming more common, and for good reason. Many years ago the prevalent philosophy was that the belay anchor was primarily a backup and that the belayer should always hold any forces that come on the system. This was also the era in which the accepted tenet was "the leader does not fall." Times have changed. Anchors are more secure. Climbers fall all the time. The new tenet is "if you're not falling, you're not pushing yourself enough." The result is that more and more climbers have discovered the many benefits of using the belay anchor as an active, front-line part of the system. It certainly makes lowering more comfortable and, often, more secure. When lowering directly from the belay anchor, be sure that:

■ the anchor is strong enough—if it is not and cannot be improved enough, do not use it directly

■ the correct belay device is used—the Petzl Gri Gri or Munter hitch is a good choice; plates and tubes should only be used if the belayer can lock them off effectively

LOWERING TO AN ANCHOR

Not all lowers end on the ground. If you want to top-rope the last pitch of The Nose on El Capitan, for instance, there will still be about 3,000 feet of air under the climber's feet when he or she reaches the end of the rope. In situations like this, the system is simple. The belayer lowers the climber to the point where he or she will begin climbing. Since the climber is already on belay, he or she simply begins climbing and the belayer takes the rope in as the climber moves upward. As was mentioned in the precautions for the top lower, be sure that if the climber cannot do the moves, the team has the equipment and expertise to have the climber ascend the rope or to create a simple raising system.

It is also possible to use lowering as part of the system to retreat from a multipitch route. For example, as a climber ascends the third pitch of a route, it begins to rain and the party must go down. The simplest and fastest retreat is for the climber to lower down to the last anchor and clip back in. The belayer would then rappel to that anchor and the party would continue their descent using whatever methods they choose. This will work fine if:

- the anchor below is fixed
- the second knows how to clip back into the anchor safely

But what if the second is a novice and is uncertain about how to clip in correctly? If the second is in clear view when he or she reaches the anchor, the belayer can coach and visually verify that the second is clipped in correctly. The second can also have slings girth-hitched to the harness and ready to be clipped in to a fixed anchor with locking carabiners. But suppose the belayer cannot visually verify that the second is clipped in

The climber is prerigged with girth-hitched slings. When the climber reaches the next two-point anchor he or she will clip a sling to each point with a locking carabiner.

correctly? Or what if the anchor was built from nuts and cams and the second cannot reconstruct it? In these cases the best option is for the leader to descend first via rappel with the second prerigged to follow. Lowering is an excellent tool, but be careful not to use it in situations in which complications could arise that you are not prepared to deal with.

DESCENDING TWO PITCHES QUICKLY

There are times when it is imperative that you are able to get someone down two pitches quickly; perhaps a climber is injured and needs to be lowered quickly to rescuers on the ground. Or, perhaps a party of three is two pitches up when the big storm comes in, and putting one person back on the ground immediately allows the remaining two climbers to do two quick rappels to get down. There are several methods for descending more than one pitch at a time; each requires that at least two ropes are tied together, and that the joining knot is passed through the system efficiently and safely.

The following two methods are the simplest and most straightforward. The first method lowers the climber down two rope lengths; in the second method, the climber rappels the first rope length and is lowered down the second. Each system requires two ropes tied together and two belay/rappel devices (a Munter hitch works well for one), and is easiest to perform directly off the anchor. These systems are relatively complex, and it must be stressed again that they should only be undertaken if no simpler or more efficient options exist.

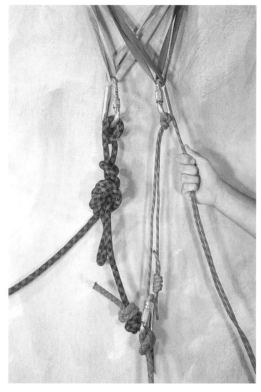

Dave's lower: The belayer has lowered the climber to the end of the first strand and is about to bump up against the knot.

The belayer has untied the overhand backup, has released the mule knot, and is lowering the first strand onto the second anchor using the Munter hitch on the cordelette.

Dave's Lower

This improved variation on the traditional knot pass is very quick and straightforward; it was developed by Dave Kelly, an American Mountain Guides Association (AMGA)–certified guide from the Eastern Mountain Sports Climbing School in North Conway, New Hampshire.

1. Attach a cordelette to a locking carabiner on the anchor with a Munter hitch, blocked with a mule knot and backed up with an overhand around the cordelette.
2. Clip a second, pear-shaped carabiner to the bottom loop of the cordelette.
3. Clip a third carabiner to the anchor and thread the second rope through it just above the joining knot using a Munter hitch, block it with a mule knot (see page 32), and back it up with an overhand loop clipped back to the anchor or tied around the rope.

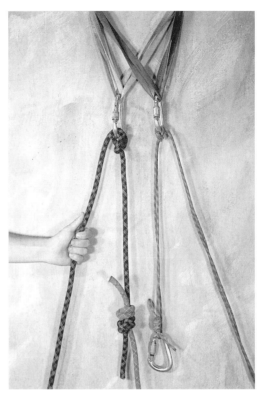

Once the load is on the second anchor, the original Munter carabiner can be twisted off the rope—yes, this can be done even under tension.

The belayer is now free to lower the climber the second rope length.

4. Have the climber being lowered tie into the free end of the first rope, and put him or her on belay through a device (or another Munter hitch) on the locking carabiner on the bottom of the cordelette.

5. Lower the climber the length of the first strand through the belay device until the joining knot jams in the carabiner.

6. Untie the overhand backup on the cordelette, release the mule knot, and lower the load onto the second belay device with the Munter hitch on the cordelette.

7. Unlock the locking carabiner between the cordelette and the rope, and twist it until it comes off the rope (it will come off, even under a load).

8. Unclip and untie the overhand backup, release the mule knot, and lower the climber the second pitch using the Munter hitch on the rope.

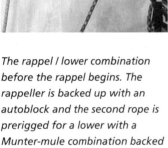

The rappel / lower combination before the rappel begins. The rappeller is backed up with an autoblock and the second rope is prerigged for a lower with a Munter-mule combination backed up with an overhand knot.

The rappeller has reached the end of the rope and the rappel device has jammed up against his tie-in knot.

The belayer has removed the overhand backup, popped the mule knot and is lowering the person the second pitch with the Munter hitch.

The Rappel/Lower Combination

This method is quick and simple, but requires that the person descending first can rappel competently and knows how to safely use an autoblock backup. Begin by tying two ropes together. The strand of rope being used first will be called the "first rope" and the one being used last will be called the "second rope."

1. Tie two ropes together and tie a knot in the free end of the second rope.
2. Thread the second rope through a belay device just above the joining knot on the ropes, block the device with a mule knot, tie an overhand backup, and clip it to the anchor with a locking carabiner.
3. The climber descending puts him or herself on rappel on the first rope just below the joining knot, establishes an autoblock backup, and rappels to the end of the rope (the climber will stop when he or she hits his or her tie-in knot).
4. The belayer now unclips and unties the overhand loop, pops the mule knot, and lowers the person down the second pitch.

KEY TRANSITION EXERCISE: LEARNING THE VITAL SKILLS FOR CLIMBING OUTSIDE
Getting Down Two Pitches Fast

THE CHALLENGE

It is sometimes critical to get to the ground quickly, and being able to descend two rope lengths at a time may be a life-saving skill.

THE DIFFERENCE BETWEEN LOWERING OR RAPPELLING TWO PITCHES INDOORS AND OUTDOORS

Indoors: You never do double-rope-length lowers or rappels indoors.

Outdoors: It is sometimes imperative for the safety of the party to get someone down really fast (for example, lower an injured person to rescuers) or to get down quickly yourself (for example, rappel two pitches to the ground without any intermediate anchor before the thunderstorm hits).

THE GOAL

Learn the simple methods of passing knots while lowering and rappelling.

THE EQUIPMENT

    1 rope
    1 cordelette
    6 locking carabiners
    4–6 24-inch slings
    1 two-point anchor

THE SETUP

Use the standard two-point anchor setup (see the How to Use This Book section in the Introduction).

Exercise for Getting Down Two Pitches Fast

This exercise teaches the basic steps in the following situations:
- lowering someone two pitches and passing a knot
- the rappel/lower combination to descend two pitches without passing a knot

Dave's Lower

1. Tie a figure eight loop in the middle of the rope to simulate a knot joining two ropes together (alternatively, you can use two ropes tied together).
2. Have each person tie in to an end of the rope.
3. The belayer ties a figure eight loop in his or her end of the rope and clips it to the anchor as his or her tie-in.

4. The belayer attaches a cordelette to a locking carabiner on the anchor with a Munter hitch, blocks it with a mule knot, and backs it up with an overhand around the cordelette.

5. Clip a second, pear-shaped carabiner to the bottom loop of the cordelette.

6. Clip a third carabiner to the anchor and thread the second rope through it just above the joining knot using a Munter hitch; block it with a mule knot and back it up with an overhand loop clipped back to the anchor or tied around the rope.

7. The belayer puts the climber on belay through a device (or another Munter hitch) on the locking carabiner on the bottom of the cordelette. The climber unties from the anchor.

8. The belayer lowers the climber the length of the first strand until the joining knot jams in the carabiner on the cordelette.

9. Untie the overhand backup on the cordelette, release the mule knot, and lower the load onto the second belay device with the Munter hitch on the cordelette.

10. Unlock the locking carabiner between the cordelette and the rope, and twist it until it comes off the rope (it will come off the rope even under tension).

11. Unclip and untie the overhand backup, release the mule knot, and lower the climber using the Munter hitch on the rope.

12. Switch positions and repeat steps 3 through 11.

The Rappel/Lower Combination

This method is very fast but requires careful setup, and the person descending must be capable of rappelling with an autoblock backup.

1. Repeat steps 1 through 3 in the Dave's Lower option, above.

2. The belayer threads the rope through a belay device just above the joining knot, clips it to the anchor, blocks it with a mule knot, and backs it up with an overhand loop clipped to the anchor with a locking carabiner.

3. The climber girth-hitches a sling to the harness, attaches a rappel device, threads it onto the rope just below the joining knot, and establishes an autoblock backup. The climber unties from the anchor.

4. The climber now rappels until he or she reaches the end of the rope; because the climber is tied in, he or she will just stop when he or she runs out of rope.

5. The belayer now unties the overhand backup, pops the mule knot, and lowers the climber until he or she reaches the ground or the next anchor.

6. Switch positions and repeat steps 2 through 7.

LOWERING BACKUPS

Climbing systems are built on redundancy, and you should always consider establishing a backup for a lower. There are situations (rain, darkness, icy rope, et cetera) in which a backup will greatly enhance security. The simplest way to back up a lower is an extra hand. When available, have a third person feed the brake side to the belayer during the lower. If the belayer loses control, the backup belayer

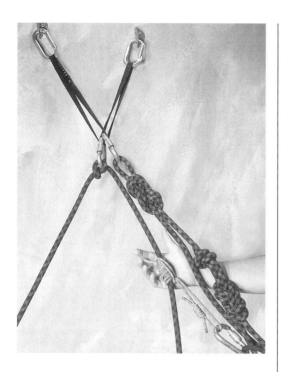

Backing up a lower off the anchor with an autoblock on the brake strand clipped to the belayer's harness.

can hold the weight of the climber and even take over the lower.

If no backup belayer is available and the lower is being done off the anchor, a simple backup can be established by attaching a prusik or similar clamping hitch to the brake strand of the rope and clipping it to the belayer's harness. The belayer's free hand can keep the hitch loose during the lower, but if anything goes wrong, it will hold the weight. (If the belayer is lowering from a device attached to his or her harness, the clamping hitch should be attached to the loaded strand instead of the brake strand and kept loose with the guide hand.)

BELAY ESCAPES

A fundamental skill in all rescue situations is the ability to safely escape the system without compromising anyone's safety. A climber doing something as simple as belaying his or her partner can become trapped in the system by an accident, which can put both their lives at risk. You can free yourself from almost any system if you have the proper equipment, are competent with the fundamental skills like belaying, and know how to:

■ tie a Munter hitch and mule knot, and use the two in combination
■ tie and use a clamping knot like the prusik or Klemheist

Just as it seems weird for a parachutist to jump out of a perfectly good airplane, it seems odd that a climber would want to leave a perfectly good belay. The reason is simple; the person climbing has somehow become incapacitated, and the need for belaying has been replaced by the need for rescuing. The typical problem is that the belayer is holding the climber's weight when the need to escape the belay arises. Thus, belay escapes usually require the same basics steps:

1. blocking the belay—this frees the belayer's hands
2. transferring the load from the original belay system to the anchor—this takes the responsibility of carrying the load away from the belayer, freeing him or her to physically leave the belay
3. backing the system up—this ensures that the system cannot fail while the belayer moves into the rescue mode
4. effecting the rescue—this can take many forms, from leaving the scene and going for help, to rigging a haul or rappel system to facilitate retreat, to ascending the rope to rescue an injured leader

The first part of this section describes the steps to escape the belay using the standard belay techniques: belaying off the anchor, redirecting the belay off the anchor, and belaying off the harness. Each escape is described to the point of having the belayer free from the system and the anchor backed up. The steps necessary for the belayer to rescue the injured climber, whether he or she is the second or the leader, are beyond the scope of this book.

OFF THE ANCHOR

This is by far the simplest belay escape scenario. When giving a top-rope belay to a climber directly off the anchor, the belayer has already accomplished step 2 in the basic process—he or she has already transferred the load to the anchor. Because this is often the most complicated, time-consuming, and dangerous step, it is one more good reason to consider belaying the second off the anchor whenever possible. Regardless of the device used—Munter hitch, Petzl Gri Gri, belay plate, or tube—the steps to escape this belay are always the same:

1. Block the belay with a mule knot.
2. Tie a backup overhand or figure eight loop and clip it to the anchor with a locking carabiner.

FROM THE HARNESS OR REDIRECTED OFF THE ANCHOR

It has always been common to belay the second off the belayer's harness. There are often better choices, and this is nowhere more evident than when escaping a belay. Until the climber's weight is successfully transferred, the belayer must hold the entire load. This often complicates the situation and can make it more dangerous.

The redirected belay, another common method, is also more complicated to escape than the belay directly off the anchor. With this

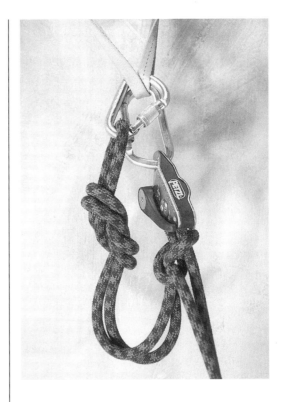

Escaping the belay off the anchor using a Gri Gri is so simple—just tie a figure eight loop, clip it to the anchor, and you're done.

method, the belay is off the harness but the rope is redirected through the anchor before going to the climber. It is easier to hold the climber's weight when escaping the redirected belay because the friction of the rope through the anchors helps carry the load.

Here are the steps for escaping a belay directly off the harness or redirected through the anchor:

1. Block the belay by tying a mule knot with the brake strand around the loaded strand—this frees the belayer's hands.
2. Attach a cordelette by tying a clamping

Escaping a top belay, step one: Tie a mule knot to block the belay and back it up with an overhand knot around the rope.

Step two: Attach a cordelette with a prusik or Klemheist hitch on the loaded strand. Step three: Clip it to the anchor with a Munter-mule combination backed up with an overhand knot.

hitch to the loaded strand (below the anchor, in the case of the redirected belay).

3. Clip the cordelette to a separate locking, pear-shaped carabiner on the anchor using the Munter-mule combination.

4. Pop the mule knot on the brake strand of the rope and lower the climber until the weight is held by the cordelette.

5. Feed 3 to 5 feet of slack through the belay device and block the original belay with another mule knot on the brake strand below the original belay device—this provides a temporary backup and ensures that the system cannot fail while the permanent backup is established.

6. Tie a figure eight on a bight in the slack rope below the anchor, and clip it to the anchor using a separate locking carabiner.

Close-up of escaping a belay.

Close-up of escaping a belay.

Step four: The belayer now removes the overhand on the rope, pops the Mule knot, and lowers the climber until the cordelette takes the load.

7. Pop the mule knot on the brake strand and remove the belay device from the system.
8. Feed rope through the figure eight on a bight on the anchor until all the slack is taken out between it and the cordelette.
9. Pop the mule knot on the cordelette and lower the climber onto the figure eight on a bight, remove the cordelette—the climber is now permanently tied off and

the belayer is free to leave the scene. (The mechanics of leaving the scene are not described here. If sufficient equipment is not available to the belayer, retreat may be difficult and dangerous.)

WHEN BELAYING THE LEADER

Suppose you are belaying the leader on a one-pitch climb, and he or she falls and cannot be lowered (for example, the leader has a broken

Step six: After the cordelette is loaded the belayer should back up the system by tying a figure eight on a bight on the rope and clipping it to the anchor as a tether (use as short a tether as possible).

Step nine: The belayer now removes the overhand backup on the cordelette, pops the mule knot, and lowers the climber using the Munter hitch until the rope takes the load. Remember, you must have a long enough cordelette to lower the climber far enough for the rope to hold the load.

Step nine continued: Once the anchor has the load the belayer can remove the cordelette and prepare to leave the belay (loaded strand on the left, belayer's tether to the anchor on the right).

leg). Help is just 5 minutes away but you have to leave the scene. How do you do it? Escaping the belay when a leader is in trouble can be straightforward or it can be desperately complicated. Again, if you know the fundamental systems, the problem can usually be solved quickly. But if you do not, you may risk your life. In the late 1990s a climber fell leading the last pitch of a long rock climb in Colorado and died from head injuries. The belayer was unable to escape the belay and held the leader all night with his brake hand. Rescuers arrived and the belayer survived, but if bad weather had come in, the belayer might have died of hypothermia just because he did not know how to tie a mule knot and transfer the load to the belay. Do not take the same risk.

The following steps assume that a good anchor is available and the belayer has the proper self-rescue equipment. If the belayer is on the ground and no anchor is available, the rescue scenario is far more complicated; those steps are not included here. Neither does this book cover the subject of how the belayer rescues an incapacitated leader. This section is limited to those circumstances in which the belayer's only responsibility is to get out of the system and go for help. Three scenarios are covered:

- the belayer is on the ground and not tied in to an anchor but one is available
- the belayer is on the ground and tied to a natural anchor such as a tree or boulder
- the belayer is tied in to a constructed anchor

Scenario 1: The belayer is on the ground and not tied in to an anchor but one is available. It is common, though not recommended, for the belayer on the ground to be unanchored when belaying the leader. Because this situation is so common, it is important to understand the steps necessary for the belayer to escape.

1. Block the belay with a mule knot backed up with an overhand knot (this frees the belayer's hands).
2. Find a secure anchor such as a tree or boulder and build an anchor—often as simple as wrapping a sling around it (if an anchor is not right next to the belayer, he or she may need to release the mule knot and "rappel" down the rope using the climber as a counterbalance in order to reach an anchor point).
3. Attach a sling or prusik loop to the loaded strand using a clamping hitch and clip it to the anchor with a locking carabiner using the Munter-mule combination.
4. Pop the mule knot on the rope and lower the climber until the clamping knot holds the load.
5. Feed 3 to 5 feet of slack through the belay device and block the original belay with another mule knot on the brake strand below the original belay device—this provides a temporary backup and ensures that the system cannot fail while the permanent backup is established.
6. Tie a figure eight on a bight in the slack rope below the belay device and clip it to the anchor using a separate locking carabiner.
7. Pop the mule knot on the brake strand and remove the belay device from the system.
8. Feed rope through the figure eight on a bight on the anchor until all the slack is taken out between it and the cordelette.
9. Pop the mule knot on the cordelette and lower the climber onto the figure eight

on a bight, then remove the cordelette—the climber is now permanently tied off and the belayer is free to leave the scene.

Scenario 2: The belayer is on the ground and tied to a natural anchor such as a tree or boulder. It is highly recommended that belayers be tied to an anchor whenever belaying a leader, even when the belayer is on the ground. By doing so, the belayer has already accomplished step 2 in the previous scenario, and can quickly accomplish step 1 and then steps 3 through 9.

Scenario 3: The belayer is tied in to a constructed anchor. In many instances (for example, on multipitch climbs), the belayer will be tied directly to an anchor constructed from either fixed hardware such as bolts or from nuts and cams. Typically, these anchors are positioned so the belayer can weight them comfortably while the leader climbs. Transferring the load created by a fallen leader to belays of this type uses the same procedures as described in Scenario 2, with one very important difference: The belay anchor must be multidirectional; it must be capable of holding a load that pulls in an upward direction. With bolts, this is no problem—they are sufficiently strong regardless of the direction of the load.

However, anchors constructed with nuts and cams are not always capable of holding an upward force. If the person building the anchor simply slotted three bomber nuts, all oriented to hold a downward force, the upward force of a fallen leader transferred to the anchor will cause it to pull out. Before using any constructed anchor, be certain it is capable of holding the anticipated load. The best constructed anchors are built multidirectionally to begin with. It is always harder, and sometimes impossible, to add components after the leader has fallen and become incapacitated—all actions must be taken while holding the fallen climber's weight, and the belayer may not even have the proper equipment to add to the belay because the leader has the rack. If the anchor cannot be made multidirectional, other rescue steps than those outlined below will have to be taken; they are beyond the scope of this book. Assuming the anchor is multidirectional, repeat the steps outlined in Scenario 2 above.

KEY TRANSITION EXERCISE: LEARNING THE VITAL SKILLS FOR CLIMBING OUTSIDE
Learning How to Escape the Belay in an Emergency

THE CHALLENGE
In an emergency, it is often necessary for the belayer to escape the belay quickly. Too often the simple skills are not known, and precious—sometimes life-saving—time is lost.

THE DIFFERENCE BETWEEN ESCAPING THE BELAY INDOORS AND ESCAPING THE BELAY OUTDOORS
Indoors: You never have to escape the belay in a gym.
Outdoors: In the case of an injured leader or second, escaping the belay is often vital to perform a rescue or get help.

THE GOAL
Master the basic, simple systems for escaping a belay when belaying a leader or second.

THE EQUIPMENT
1 rope
1 cordelette
1 two-point anchor
2–4 24-inch slings
4 locking carabiners

Note: In order to perform any basic rescue technique, including belay escapes, the belayer should always have the minimum hardware: a cordelette, several slings, rappel rings, and locking carabiners. Without them the rescue options will be severely limited.

THE SETUP
Use the standard two-point anchor setup (see the How to Use This Book section in the Introduction).

The Belay Escape Exercise
Belay escapes are only necessary when the climber, whether leader or second, is injured, nonambulatory, and usually uncommunicative. If the climber is injured but conscious and ambulatory, then in most instances he or she can be lowered back to the last belay anchor (an exception is if a leader has fallen when more than half of the rope has been used). Escaping the belay is only necessary when the climber cannot help at all. As with any rescue technique, do only what is absolutely necessary. Rescue techniques add a layer of danger to any system. Do not do a belay escape if your partner has only a sprained ankle. (Self-rescue is a complex subject and only the most basic belay escapes are demonstrated here. Refer to in-depth rescue manuals for advanced techniques.) This exercise teaches the basic steps to escape a belay in the following situations:

- when belaying a second off the harness
- when belaying a second off the anchor
- when belaying a leader off the harness

All belay escapes share the same basic steps:

1. Lock off the belay to free the belayer's hands.
2. Transfer the climber's weight to the anchor.
3. Create a secure backup.
4. Leave the belay.

Belaying the Second Off the Harness or Redirected Off the Anchor
These are the steps for escaping the belay when belaying a second.

1. Have the climber and the belayer each tie in to an end of the rope.
2. The belayer ties a figure eight loop on his or her rope and clips in to the master point of the anchor with a locking carabiner.
3. The belayer puts the climber on belay through a conventional tube or plate device clipped to the harness.
4. The climber weights the system, and the belayer locks the belay device off and holds the climber's weight.
5. The belayer ties a mule knot around the rope to temporarily lock the belay so he or she can use both hands.
6. The belayer ties an overhand loop with the brake strand around the loaded strand to back up the mule knot.
7. The belayer puts the cordelette on the loaded strand below the mule knot (below the anchor if the belay has been redirected) using a prusik or Klemheist hitch.
8. A locking carabiner is clipped to the anchor, and the other end of the cordelette is clipped to it using a Munter hitch followed by a mule knot and overhand backup (move the prusik up the rope as far as possible to give the most usable slack to the cordelette).
9. The belayer now unties the overhand backup on the climbing rope, releases the mule knot on the rope, and lowers the climber until the cordelette takes the load.
10. The belayer ties a figure eight loop on the brake side of the belay device and clips it to the anchor with a locking carabiner.
11. The belayer unties the overhand loop on the cordelette, releases the mule knot, and lowers the climber back onto the anchor using the Munter hitch.

    Note: The distance between the prusik knot and the figure eight on the rope that is clipped to the anchor must be less than the distance between the prusik and the end of the cordelette; if not, the belayer will run out of cordelette before the load comes back on the rope.
12. The belayer unties from the rope and is free from the belay.

    Note: What happens now depends on the circumstance, the skill of the belayer, and the equipment available. The possible next steps are beyond the scope of this book.
13. Switch positions and repeat steps 1 through 12.

Off the Anchor

Belay escapes when belaying off the anchor are usually far simpler than those performed when belaying off the harness, because the belayer is already out of the system and a transfer of the load is not needed. All that needs to be done is to lock off the belay and back up the system.

   Note: These steps will also work if belaying off a remote anchor or from an extended master point.

Using a Munter Hitch

This also works using a plate or tube on an extended master-point anchor.

1. Repeat steps 1 through 4 in the Belaying a Second Off the Harness option above.
2. Tie a mule knot to lock the belay. (If belaying from a remote anchor, the belayer will have to go back to the anchor first.)
3. Tie a figure eight loop and clip it to the anchor with a locking carabiner to back up the system.
4. The belayer unties from the rope and is free from the belay.
5. Switch positions and repeat steps 1 through 4.

Using a Petzl Gri Gri

1. Repeat steps 1 through 4 in the Belaying a Second Off the Harness option above.
2. The Gri Gri automatically locks up; tie a figure eight loop and clip it back to the anchor with a locking carabiner.
3. The belayer unties from the rope and is free from the belay.
4. Switch positions and repeat steps 1 through 3.

Belaying a Leader Off the Harness

The procedure for escaping the belay when a leader has fallen is exactly the same as when belaying the second, although the circumstances may be complicated on a multipitch climb. On a single-pitch climb with the belayer anchored to something on the ground (for example, a tree) below and behind him or her, the procedure is precisely the same as described in the first option above. On a multipitch climb, however, the anchor is usually above and in front of the belayer. If the anchor has not been constructed with a sufficiently strong upward component, then it will not be able to hold the weight of the leader. This is a good argument for building all anchors so they are capable of being stressed upward. In the case of a fallen leader wherein a belay escape is necessary, the anchor must be capable of taking the upward load. If it has not been constructed properly, then it is up to the belayer to modify it before transferring the load. If the equipment is not available to do this (the leader usually has all the equipment, after all), then escaping the belay safely may be impossible and another rescue technique will have to be used. Such a rescue scenario is beyond the scope of this book.

To simulate escaping the belay when a leader has fallen and the belay is as would be found on a multipitch climb (in other words, above and in front of the belayer), repeat steps 1 through 12 in the first option described above, Belaying a Second Off the Harness, but redirect the rope through a point above to simulate the upward pull.

GOING UP TO GET DOWN

Sometimes the fastest way down is to go up. Imagine for a moment that you are belaying your partner up the last 20 feet of a six-pitch route. The trail back to the car is just a few feet away, and you will easily make the car by dark. Suddenly your partner shouts up to you that he is stuck. He tries the move again, but just cannot do it. He is too tired. You could lower him back to the last belay and then begin the long series of rappels back down, but it will be dark in an hour, you do not have your headlamps, and, unfortunately, you have only one rope. You could have him climb the rope—but he does not know how. So the two of you just sit there, wondering what to do.

Imagine it starts raining. The wind starts blowing. It gets dark. No one hears you yelling for help. The rain turns to sleet. Assuming you live through the night, what will you do in the morning?

The possibilities are frightening. Though you are only imagining this scenario, for two climbers out there it was almost a memory. But the rescue team showed up before dark and it did not rain. The climbers were lucky.

In this chapter we have looked at ways to get out of trouble by rappelling, lowering, or escaping the belay. Now we look at how to get out of trouble by ascending the rope. This simple skill can help you overcome minor obstacles such as the one in the story above. Other than ascending the rope, there are many methods for creating raising systems that can pull an exhausted or injured climber up a cliff. They can be complicated and are beyond the scope of this book. For situations in which a raising system is needed to move a climber or evacuate someone who is severely injured, please consult books that cover the topic in depth.

Going up is always harder than going down. Unlike rappelling or lowering, the climber ascending the rope must fight gravity all the way. The best improvised ascending technique is the one that is avoided. If you are prepared and use good judgment, you will minimize the possibility that you will ever have to ascend the rope.

- Climb within your limits. Do not try routes that are too far above the team's ability level—if one of you climbs 5.12 but the other only 5.9, do not go up on a multipitch 5.11.

- Protect traverses well, even if they are easy. Any fall on a traverse can injure the climber or may put him or her on much more difficult ground; if he or she cannot climb back up to the route or ascend the rope, a very difficult raising system may have to be used.

- Place extra protection on sections where the second may have trouble, and leave long slings hanging from each piece. The second will easily be able to step in them or pull on them and move past the difficulties (had the leader in the opening story done this, the hard move would have been nothing but a speed bump for the second).

- Do not let your partner get so exhausted that the only recourse is to use a raising system. Give tight belays and assistance if it is clear that the move is too hard; it is better to give a little help than to have the party get stuck.

- Always be attentive when belaying the second. Too much slack at the wrong time may mean a broken ankle and the need for a rescue.

IMPROVISED ASCENDING

Being able to climb the rope itself—even if for just a few feet—can get you out of many jams. Improvised ascending uses clamping hitches on slings or cordelettes to make a way for you to climb directly up a rope. The steps are often as simple as these:

1. Have your partner lock off the belay.
2. Wrap a sling around the rope above you

using a prusik or Klemheist hitch.

3. Step up in the sling or pull on it to reach the good holds above the difficult move.

4. Have your partner pull up the slack as soon as you step out of the sling.

If a longer distance needs to be ascended, then the following simple system can be used. Have the belayer fix the belay rope to the anchor rather than lock off the belay while you climb the rope (increased comfort for the belayer and a possible increase in security—it may be difficult for him or her to hold you for the duration of the improvised ascent). The belayer can do this by blocking the belay using a mule knot with an overhand knot backup. To ascend the rope:

1. Girth-hitch two 24-inch slings together, then attach to the rope with a prusik or Klemheist hitch.

2. Clip the lower sling to your harness with a locking carabiner or two carabiners reversed and opposed—the friction hitch should be no farther than an arm's length above you (you will hang off this sling while you move your foot loops up).

3. Make a pair of foot loops with either four slings or a cordelette: To use slings, girth-hitch two 24-inch slings together and attach them to the rope with a friction hitch below the slings attached to your harness, then girth-hitch two additional 24-inch slings to the lower sling; with a cordelette, attach it to the rope below your harness slings and then tie two overhand loops in the bottom—one for each foot. For maximum efficiency, your feet should be fairly high when the friction hitch on the foot loops is slid up toward the friction hitch on your harness loops. If your feet are too low, tie overhand knots in the sling or cordelette

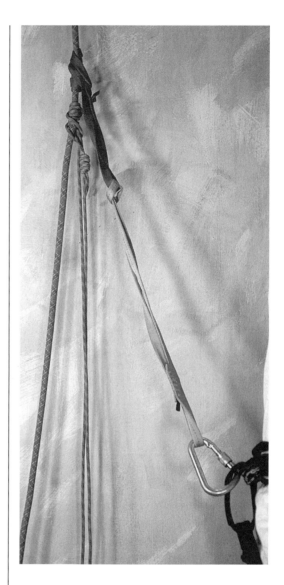

A double-length sling is attached to the rope with a Klemheist hitch and clipped to the harness with a locking carabiner—the climber will hang from this sling while moving his or her foot loops up. A cordelette is attached to the rope with a second Klemheist below the first.

The climber is hanging off the harness and his feet are in the foot loops in the bottom of the cordelette.

above the foot loops to shorten it.

4. Ascend the rope: Hang from the harness loops, slide the foot loops up, grab the rope as high up as you can, stand up, slide your harness loops up, and then hang again; repeat until you have passed the difficulty or have reached the belay anchor. If you reach a point where you can climb again, take your weight off the rope, loosen the friction hitches on the slings, and hold them loosely while the belayer re-establishes an active belay and takes up all the slack. When the slack is out of the system, remove the slings from the rope and continue climbing.

5. As you ascend, consider tying figure-eight loops every few feet and clipping them to your harness with a locking carabiner as a backup.

Glossary

active protection A protection device with moving parts; *see also* Spring Loaded Camming Device (SLCD)

adjustable harness A harness on which the size of the waist belt and leg loops can be adjusted with buckles

aid climbing Pulling on protection to make upward progress on a climb

alpine harness A harness on which the leg loops are formed by connecting straps to the waist belt

American Triangle A dangerous webbing anchor formed by threading a single piece of webbing through two anchors and tying the ends together, forming a triangle whose vectors multiply the force on the anchors; commonly found on fixed anchors, often without rappel rings

AMGA American Mountain Guides Association, a national nonprofit organization that trains and certifies professional mountain guides and accredits guiding companies

anchor Any temporary, secure point that a climber uses to protect him or herself from injury during a fall; usually capable of holding several thousand pounds; can come in many forms, including trees, boulders, pitons, bolts, nuts, camming devices, et cetera

arm bar A technique for climbing offwidth cracks by inserting the arm straight into a crack and applying counter-pressure between the palm and elbow

autoblock A clamping hitch with low holding power; often used to provide a self-belay for rappelling

back-clip Clipping the rope into a protection carabiner so that the rope could fall across the gate during a fall and accidentally open it

backstepping Using your foot on its outside edge with your knee bent inward

backup belayer A second person who feeds the rope to the primary belayer; he or she will lock off the belay if the primary belayer loses control

belay Means "to hold"; refers to a system of devices and techniques that combine to protect a climber from being injured in a fall by locking the rope

belay anchor Any single-point or multipoint anchor from which a belay is made

belay device Any of several devices that are used to create a bend in the rope that provides manageable friction for belaying or rappelling

belay escape Any of several methods that allow the belayer to tie off a fallen climber and physically leave the system

belay loop A sewn loop on the front of some harnesses; used for belaying and rappelling

bent-gate carabiner A carabiner whose gate is bent inward to facilitate clipping in the rope

big-wall climbing Multiday climbing on huge cliffs; often includes aid climbing techniques

bight Any bend in the rope that does not cross itself; used in many knots and to thread belay/rappel devices

blocking knot A knot used to maintain the integrity of a system or temporarily hold weight

board-lasted A shoe constructed around a stiff midsole

bolt An anchor point consisting of a metal shaft that is placed in a drilled hole and is held there by either friction or epoxy; an accompanying hanger provides an attachment point, strongest when loaded perpendicular to the shaft

bombproof A completely reliable anchor; also called a bomber

bouldering Low-to-the-ground climbing wherein the climber can jump back down to the ground, and a rope and belay are not necessary

braced stance A belay position wherein the belayer's body is positioned so that it is able to hold a fall without additional anchors

brake hand The hand that holds the rope on the side of the belay device opposite the climber and that will activate the locking mechanism; the brake hand never leaves the rope

brake strand The strand of rope on the brake-hand side of the belay

butterflying the rope A method for temporarily storing the rope in which loops are dropped alternately over the belayer's tether

cam Generic term for Spring Loaded Camming Device (SLCD)

carabiner An aluminum snap-link used to connect parts of a climbing system

CATCH A set of belaying principles: **C**losed system, **A**ligned and **T**ight to the anchor, **C**ommunication clear, and brake **H**and on the rope

chalk Gymnastic chalk used by climbers to keep their fingers dry

chicken wing A technique for climbing off-width cracks by inserting the arm bent at the elbow into a crack and using counter-pressure between the forearm and upper arm

chock Generic for "artificial chockstone," any of many designs of passive protection that rely on wedging in a constriction for security: hexes, stoppers, tricams, et cetera

chockstone A stone wedged in a crack

clamping hitch Any of several hitches that will tighten and lock when loaded; most often used on a rope to temporarily hold a load; also called a friction hitch

class A rating system from 1 to 6 that describes general difficulty, ranging from hiking to aid climbing

cleaning To remove protection from a climb

closed system A contained system; the belayer tying in to the end of the rope forms a "closed system" that will keep the climber from being dropped; the magic **X** forms a "closed system" wherein the master point is attached to the sling and not merely looped over it

clove hitch A hitch used to tie off parts of a

system; often used by the climber to clip into the belay

cord Nylon fibers woven like a rope using Kernmantle construction, typically 5.5 mm to 8 mm in diameter; used tied in short loops as clamping hitches

cordelette A 6- to 9-foot loop of cord usually between 5.5 mm and 8 mm in diameter tied with a double or triple fisherman knot; has many uses, including building belay anchors and as a component of self-rescue systems

core The climbing rope's central core of woven nylon fibers; accounts for about 85 percent of the rope

crack climbing Climbing utilizing the natural fissures in the rock for hand- and footholds

crimp A small handhold in which the fingers are hyperextended

crunch The position in which the feet are held high and the hands low

crux The hardest move or series of moves on a pitch; the hardest pitch on a multipitch climb

directional Any auxiliary anchor point used to position the rope in the strongest possible location

double fisherman A standard knot for joining two ropes together; knots are tied on each strand that jam together under a load

double-pass buckle The standard harness buckle; requires the waist-belt webbing to be threaded through twice, crossing over itself and locking on the second pass

dressing The act of making a knot neat and tight

dynamic move A move wherein the climber moves aggressively toward a hold and will fall off if he or she does not grab it securely; *see also* static move

dynamic rope A climbing rope that is designed to stretch considerably and absorb the force of a falling climber; the only kind of rope suitable for leading

edging Using the inside or outside edge of the shoe on a protruding hold

equalization Any of several methods that tie anchors together in such a way that they share a load equally

ERNEST A set of principles for constructed belay anchors: Equalized, Redundant, No Extension, Strong and Stable, Timely

extended master point Belaying off a master point that is not in direct proximity to the belay anchor itself

extension A potential slipping of components in an anchor system to adjust for the failure of any point; causes an undesirable shock load

face climbing Climbing technique that uses small ledges for hand- and footholds

fall factor A measure of the severity of a fall; derived by dividing the length of the fall into the length of rope in the system: the maximum fall factor is 2

fall line A line parallel to that of gravity

figure eight device An aluminum rappel and belay device in the shape of an 8

figure eight knot A knot shaped like an 8; has many uses, including connecting the rope to the harness, tying into an anchor, tying two ropes together, tied on a bight to form a loop, et cetera

finger crack A crack large enough to just admit the fingers or part of the fingers

fireman's belay A rappel belay created by having a person at the bottom of a pitch hold the rappel rope in his or her hand; keeping the rope slack allows the rappeller to descend, pulling down on the rope locks off the rappel

fist crack A crack large enough for the fist to be jammed in it

fix To anchor something either temporarily or permanently

fixed anchor Any permanent anchor point; can be natural, like a tree, or manufactured, like a bolt or piton

fixed leg loops A harness style wherein the leg loops are permanently sewn and cannot be adjusted

fixed protection Pitons, bolt, nuts, or cams (SLCDs) that are left permanently in place

flagging Using the weight of one foot and leg, in the air, to help maintain balance while making a move with the other foot and leg

foot stack Jamming both feet together in a crack too large to be jammed with just one foot

forest duff Decomposing leaves, sticks, needles, and other tree and plant debris; forms the basis for many forest soils; trees growing in duff on ledges are notoriously weak anchors

free carabiner A carabiner carried on the rack by itself with nothing clipped to it

free climbing Climbing wherein the hands and feet are used alone to make progress, and climbing equipment is used only to provide protection in the case of a fall; *see also* soloing

friction climbing Climbing that relies on the friction of the bottom of the shoe for security on smooth rock where no obvious footholds exist

friction wrap A technique for creating a belay anchor wherein the rope is wrapped, often several times, around a tree and uses the friction alone for security

front-pointing Using the toe of the shoe placed straight onto a foothold

gaston A side-pull hold in front of the body, held with the thumb down

gate flutter The fast, repeated opening and closing of a carabiner gate that can occur when the rope runs through it during a fall

girth hitch A hitch used to tie off parts of a system in which one end of a sling is run through the other end while being wrapped around something

grade A rating system of I through VII that describes the approximate time (commitment) it will take to climb a route, from a couple of hours to several days

Gri Gri An auto-locking belay device made by Petzl

guide hand The hand opposite the brake hand; helps position and manage the rope

hand crack A crack that is large enough for the hands to be inserted to form hand jams

hand jam A crack-climbing technique in which the hand is flexed inside a crack to form a hold

hand stack An offwidth climbing technique in which both hands are jammed together in a crack that is too wide to be jammed with just one hand

hangdog To work the moves on a route by resting on the rope between attempts

hanging belay A belay stance without a ledge to stand on, wherein the climbers must hang in their harnesses

hex A nonsymmetrical, five-sided chock with varying degrees of camming action

highstep A move wherein the next foothold is above the waist

hitch A connection like a knot but wherein the integrity of the system relies on the thing being hitched; a hitch, unlike a knot, will not stand alone

HMS carabiner A large, pear-shaped carabiner with a large, round curve on the end opposite the gate; the only type of carabiner that should be used with the Munter hitch

horn A spike of rock

impact force The force still remaining when a falling climber comes to a stop; in a severe fall it can be a maximum of 2,680 pounds

improvised ascending Any of various methods of ascending a fixed rope without the use of mechanical rope clamps

inside corner A place where two planes of rock intersect at an angle of less than 180 degrees

jamming Placing hands or feet in a crack to gain a secure hold

keeper cord A short cord attached to a belay/rappel device; it keeps the device within reach when in use, and clips the device to a carabiner when not in use

keeper knot Any auxiliary knot used to ensure the security of another knot; for example, a half double fisherman knot tied after a figure eight tie-in is a keeper knot

Kernmantle Means "core and sheath" and is the method by which climbing ropes are constructed

Kevlar™ A synthetic material that is used to make cord and some climbing accessories

kilonewton A measurement of force; abbreviated kN

Klemheist One of several clamping hitches used to back up systems or gain a hold on a rope

knot pass Any of several systems used to pass a knot through a belay system

lap coil A coil that consists of overlapping loops, typically tied off so it can be carried like a backpack; is less likely to tangle when being uncoiled for use

lap link An open, steel ring with overlapping ends that are hammered together after the ring is placed around something; often used as the master point on fixed belay anchors; also called a lowering ring

lead climbing A system of climbing from the ground up wherein a climber ascends while belayed from below by a partner, trailing a

rope and clipping it through intermediate protection points; when the leader reaches the end of a pitch, he or she will anchor the rope and belay up the second climber on a top-rope; the process is then repeated until the top of a climb is reached

leader The person leading a pitch; also called the lead climber

lead fall A fall taken while leading; in the case of a lead fall, the belayer will hold the fall, which will be caught by the last piece of protection

Leave No Trace A nonprofit organization that promotes a low-impact environmental ethic of the same name

leg loops The part of the harness that goes around the legs

lieback A hold that is oriented vertically and pulled on sideways; also called a side pull

live end The end of the rope tied to the climber

locking carabiner A carabiner with any of various locking mechanisms that keep the gate from opening unexpectedly

lock off A body position in which the climber holds him or herself in place with one arm fully contracted

loop A bend in rope or webbing that crosses over itself

lowering A method of descent wherein the climber weights the rope and is let down by the belayer; the common method of descent from a slingshot belay

lowering ring *see also* lap link

magic X A method for creating a self-equalizing master point by tying two anchor points together with a sling loop; a half-twist in one strand of the sling creates a closed system ensuring that the master point cannot come off the rope if either anchor point fails

mantle A series of moves that allow the climber to stand up on a foothold; similar to the movement used to climb out of a swimming pool

master point The central attachment point in a belay anchor

mule knot A blocking knot that can be released under tension; used in many self-rescue applications

multidirectional An anchor that is secure in any direction

multipitch A climb that is longer than the length of a climbing rope and must be climbed in stages

Munter hitch A hitch that binds on itself, creating manageable friction; used for belaying and rappelling

Munter-mule Using the Munter hitch and mule knot in combination; foundational to many self-rescue systems

nut Generic term for any piece of passive protection

nut pick A thin metal pick used to help loosen and remove protection or to clean cracks

objective hazard A hazard that cannot be controlled by the climber: rockfall, lightning, et cetera

off fingers A crack that is too big for fingers and too small for hands

off hands A crack that is too big for hands and too small for fists

offwidth crack A crack that is too big for fists and too small for the entire body

on a bight A knot tied in the middle of a rope

on-sight To lead a route on the first try without falling

open grip A handhold in which the fingers are not hyperextended

opposition Using opposing forces for strength; usually refers to two pieces of protection that are placed to hold force in opposite directions and tied together to form one multidirectional anchor

outside corner/arête Two planes of rock that meet to form a pointed edge

overhand backup An overhand knot tied on a bight to form a loop that is clipped in to the system as a backup

overhanging Any section of rock that is steeper than vertical

palming Using the palm of the hand as a friction hold

passive protection A protection device without moving parts; *see also* chock, nut

perlon A type of nylon used in climbing cordage such as ropes and slings

pinch grip A handhold in which the fingers and thumb work in opposition to pinch a hold

pitch A section of a climb whose maximum length is dictated by the length of the rope, usually 165 feet (50 m); all top-rope climbs are one pitch

piton Any of several designs of steel spikes from the size of a postage stamp to 6 inches that are hammered into cracks to create an anchor; an eye on the piton provides an attachment point; pitons are usually loaded perpendicular to the long axis

pocket A hole in the rock that forms a hand- or foothold; often found in gyms, common in limestone

prerigged rappel A rappel system wherein each person's rappel is established on the rope, one on top of the other, prior to the first person rappelling

protection A single anchor that the rope runs freely through to protect a climber during a lead

prusik A clamping hitch used in belay and self-rescue systems

quickdraw A short sling with a carabiner clipped to each end

rack The climber's collection of protection, slings, quickdraws, et cetera

rand The outside portion of the shoe that runs around the shoe just above the sole; usually made of rubber in a climbing shoe

rappel Any of various methods of descending a rope using controlled friction

rappel anchor Any anchor used as the master point for a rappel

rappel ring/link A permanent ring or lap link found at the master point of a fixed anchor, through which the rope is threaded for rappelling or lowering

ratchet A one-way locking mechanism used to hold a load while it is repositioned

redirect Changing the direction of a vector by rerouting it; can increase control; for example, running the rope from the belayer's device through an anchor before going to the climber

redpoint To climb a route without falling after repeated tries

redundancy A principle of climbing that builds extra equipment into a system as a backup

remote master point A system for belaying wherein the device used to belay is attached directly to the anchor and is operated by the belayer from a distance

rest position To hang straight-armed off a high hold to conserve energy

reversed and opposed A method for using two carabiners together so they are oriented with their gates opening in opposite directions and on opposite sides; used any time maximum security is required

rope bag A nylon sack used to carry the rope; opens to form a mat on which the rope can be stacked on the ground

rope drag Friction caused by the rope running through parts of the system

round coil A way of coiling the climbing rope in a traditional circular coil; usually carried over the head and one shoulder

R rating A seriousness rating that indicates the route has sparse or insecure protection, and a climber could be injured in a fall

run-out Used to describe a climb that has protection that is spaced widely apart

RURP Realized Ultimate Reality Piton; a tiny piton not much bigger than a postage stamp

sandbag To mislead someone regarding the difficulty or danger of a route; potentially dangerous

second The climber who will follow the leader up a pitch, cleaning the protection as he or she goes

seconding The act of following and cleaning a pitch

SECURE A set of belay anchor principles for a top-rope anchor: **S**trong, **E**xtended over the edge, **C**entered over the climb, **U**nbroken ring as the master point, rope **R**uns easily, **E**dge padded

self-equalizing An anchor that maintains equalization automatically when its master point is repositioned; the magic **X** is a self-equalizing anchor

self-rescue Any rescue system utilizing only the climbing equipment that the climbers on the scene possess

sewing machine legs Involuntary shaking of the legs due to nervousness

sheath The woven nylon outer layer of a rope that protects the core from damage; accounts for about 15 percent of the strength of the rope

single rope A climbing rope rated to be used as a single strand between climbers

SLCD Acronym for Spring Loaded Camming Device; describes the design of several brands of active protection that use spring-loaded cams to create an anchor in a crack

slings Webbing tied into a loop; typically 4 inches to 4 feet long

slingshot The standard system for top-roping wherein the rope is doubled through an anchor at the top of the route and the climber is belayed from on the ground

slip-lasted A shoe that is not constructed around a stiff midsole; *see also* board-lasted

slippers Thin, lightweight climbing shoes, usually without laces, that offer great sensitivity but almost no support

smear A foothold in which the entire bottom of the front of the shoe is pasted on a smooth section of rock

soloing Climbing without a belay; a fall can be, and often is, fatal

Spectra™ A synthetic material used to make cord or webbing and used in many climbing applications

spider A self-rescue system that hangs two or more climbers off the same cordelette or sling simultaneously

sport climbing Climbing, indoors or out, in which all the protection and anchors are permanently in place

spotting Giving protection to a climber climbing close to the ground by standing under him or her and using outstretched arms to help cushion a fall; often used when bouldering

squeeze chimney A chimney small enough to just barely admit the climber's body

stacking the rope Uncoiling the rope into a loose pile with a top and bottom exposed; the climber ties in to the top end; minimizes tangles

standing end The opposite end of the rope from the one the climber is tied to; *see also* live end

static elongation The amount a rope will stretch when holding a body-weight load

static move A move wherein the climber moves slowly and in control and will not fall off if the next hold is not grabbed securely; *see also* dynamic move

static rope A climbing rope that is designed to stretch little and is used in situations wherein only body-weight loads are expected, such as rappelling, ascending fixed ropes, et cetera

stemming A climbing technique wherein opposing footholds are pushed off from each other for security; often used in inside corners

stick-clip To clip the rope to a bolt by attaching a carabiner or quickdraw to a long stick; useful to get the rope through the first piece of protection on sport routes

stopper Any of several wedge-shaped chocks designed to fit constrictions in cracks

stopper knot A knot tied in the end of a rope or sling to keep something else from sliding off it

straight-gate carabiner A carabiner with a straight gate

subjective hazard A hazard that can be controlled by the climber; for example, a sharp edge that can be padded

tail The amount of rope sticking out after a knot is tied

talus Large rocks (6 inches or bigger) that are often present on the slopes underneath cliffs; caution is required while moving over talus because the stability varies

test-fall The laboratory fall used by the UIAA to test ropes; a 16.5-foot fall on 8.25 feet of rope

tether The short section of rope formed when the climber ties a figure eight on a bight and clips in to the anchor; length varies depending on the situation; also called a leash

third class Slang for soloing; to "third class" a route is to demote its grade to that of a third-class route, which does not require a rope

thread Any naturally occurring tunnel in the rock that a sling may be passed through and used as an anchor (if strong enough)

top-lower To lower a climber from above

top-rope anchor The belay anchor for a top-rope

top-rope fall A fall while climbing on a top-rope; usually very short unless there is slack in the system

top-roping Any of several systems wherein the climber is protected from falling by an overhead belay

torquing Twisting hands, fingers, or feet to increase the security of a jam

traditional climbing A climbing system wherein the protection points and belay anchors that are placed in the rock while climbing the route are removed by the second

tramming A system that uses a quickdraw on the climber's harness clipped to the rope running between the top anchor and the base of the route; keeps the climber within reach of the rock while being lowered on overhanging or traversing routes

transition The steps required to change from one fundamental system to another; for example, from climbing to rappelling

traverse Any part of a climb that moves sideways rather than up

tri-axial loading A dangerous situation that arises when a carabiner is stressed by three vectors, one of which is not aligned with the carabiner's long axis; weakens the carabiner and can cause failure if shock-loaded

Tricam A single cam with a pivot point, opposing rails, and a fixed sling that follows the curve of the cam between the rails; works by camming or wedging in a crack or pocket

tubular webbing Webbing woven so that it has a circular cross section

UIAA The Union Internationale des Associations Alpines; the international agency that sets standards for and tests climbing safety equipment

undercling A hold that is oriented so that it is best when pulled up on

unidirectional An anchor that is secure in only one direction

"up rope" A command made by the climber asking for slack to be removed from the system

vector Any quantity with both magnitude and direction (for example, a climber hanging on a rope forms a vector between him or herself and the anchor)

waist belay A belay method that uses the belayer's body to create the friction necessary to hold the climber; its use is limited to low-load situations

walking The tendency for SLCDs to creep, cams first, into a crack when lateral force is applied to their stem; can compromise the security of the placement and can be minimized by using a sling extension

water knot The standard knot used to connect webbing; a retraced overhand knot

webbing Nylon fibers woven flat like a strap; used for making slings

wire-gate carabiner A carabiner whose gate is made of wire instead of solid aluminum stock

X rating A seriousness rating that indicates a climb has such sparse or insecure protection that a falling leader could be killed

Yosemite Decimal System American rock-climbing rating system (abbreviated YDS); rates the difficulty of individual Class 5 moves on a scale from 5.0 to 5.14; routes above 5.10 are further broken down into subratings *a* through *d* (for example, 5.12a)

zipper effect Protection that pulls out during a fall as a result of being levered out of place when slings of adequate length are not used

Index

A

Access Fund 65
active protection 92-94
aerobic training 51
aid climbing 37
Ament, Pat 16
American Mountain Guides Association
   (AMGA) 154
American Triangle 141
approaches and descents 62, 64
arm bar (*see also* offwidth cracks) 117-119
autoblock hitch,
      described 33, 34, 35
      to back up a rappel 76, 77, 133, 134, 143-
         145, 147, 149, 156

B

back clipping 85
backstepping 56, 57
belay anchors 26, 96-113, 152
      centered over climb 96, 97
      extended over edge 96
belay escapes 125-127, 159-168
      off the anchor 160, 166-168
      off the harness or redirected 160-163
      when belaying the leader 163-165, 168
belay/rappel device (*see also* Gri Gri)
      described 23, 24, 26,
      when belaying the second 124-127
      when lowering 152
belaying 46-48, 67-70, 72, 84, 85, 124-131
      a rappel 133
      backup belaying 158
      off an extended master point 127, 128,
         129-131
      off the anchor 125, 126, 129-131
      off the harness 124, 125, 129-131
      redirected off the anchor 126, 127, 129-
         131
      the leader 84, 85
      belay loop 46
bent-gate carabiner 24, 26, 27, 90
bight 30
board-lasted 19, 20
bolts 62, 71, 74, 90-91
bouldering 39, 50, 54, 81
brake hand 46-48, 70, 141, 142
butterflying the rope 134, 135

C

cams (*see* SLCD's)

carabiner 24-27, 89, 90

CATCH principles 67-70, 84, 124, 152

chalk 29

chicken wing (*see also* offwidth cracks) 118, 119

chock (*see* nut)

chockstones 91

clamping hitch (*see also* autoblock hitch, hitch, Klemheist hitch, and prusik hitch)

    described 33-35

    used as when working near the edge 102

    used as a lowering backup 158

    used during belay escapes 159-164

    used for improvised ascending 169-171

class 37, 38

cleaning a toprope 74-78

climbing ethics 66

climbing moves 39-45, 114-119

climbing training 53

closed system 67, 102, 151

clothing 28, 29

clove hitch 33, 34

communication 70, 72, 151

constructed anchors 105, 108-113, 165

cord 27, 28

cordelette,

    described 27, 31, 95, 131

    used to create belay anchors 112, 113

    used in self rescue systems 139, 154, 160-163, 170

crack climbing (*see also* jamming) 114-118

    finger cracks 114, 115

    hand cracks, 114-116

    fist cracks, 114, 116

    offwidth cracks 114, 117, 118

    chimney cracks 114, 118

crimp 39, 58

crunch 44

D

D carabiner 25, 26, 89, 90

Dave's Lower 154, 155, 157, 158

double fisherman knot 31

double ropes 17, 23, 32

double-pass buckle 23

dressing 30

dynamic move (*compare to* static move) 43

E

Eastern Mountain Sports Climbing School 154

edges, padding 97, 98

edging 43

endurance training 53, 54, 58, 59

environmental concerns 65

equalization 105

ERNEST principles 105, 108-113

ethics 66

etiquette 65, 66

extension 105, 108

F

fall factor 18

fall line 142

falling objects 64, 65

figure eight device 23

figure eight follow-through knot 30

figure eight on a bight knot 30, 31, 79, 80, 105, 127, 162-164

fingerboard training 58, 59

fireman's belay 133, 134, 142, 146

fixed anchors 70, 71, 74,

    evaluating 90-91

flagging 44, 45, 56

foot stack 117

footholds 43-45, 114

free climbing 37

friction wrap 101, 102, 103, 107

Friends 92

front pointing 43

G
gaston 40
gate flutter 24
girth hitch 32, 34, 98-100, 132, 133, 153
grade 36
Gri Gri 23, 24, 49, 126, 152, 160, 168
guide hand 46, 48
guidebook 71, 95
gyms, history 12, 13

H
handholds 39-43
hangdogging 54
hanging belay 128
harness 21-23
    adjustable 22
    alpine 21
    fixed leg loops 21, 2
    hazard assessment 62-65
helmet 20, 21, 66, 1 51
highstep 44, 45
hitch 30 (*see also* clamping hitches)
HMS carabiner 26, 32

I
impact force 17, 18
improvised ascending 169-171
injury prevention 50-52, 58

J
jamming (*see also* crack climbing) 41, 57, 58,
    114-119
Jardine, Ray 92

K
Kelly, Dave ??
Kevlar™ 27, 31
Kilonewton 25
Klemheist hitch 33, 34,
    used in self rescue systems 159, 161,
    used in improvised ascending 169-171

Kor, Layton 16

L
lap link (see rappel ring)
lead climbing 83-85, 120-124, 134, 135
lead fall 18
leading 84, 120-124
Leave No Trace 65
leg loop 21, 22
lieback 41, 42
live end 30, 46
lock off 41, 42
locking carabiner 25, 26, 27
loop 30
lowering 49, 73, 75, 76, 132, 133, 150-159
    backups 158, 159
    passing a knot 154, 155, 157, 158

M
magic **X** 100, 101, 108, 110-112
mantle 40, 41
master point 71, 81, 96, 100-103, 105, 108, 110-
    112, 127, 128, 141
matching 41
mule knot 154-156, 159-164
Mule knot 32, 33, 160-163, 170
multi-directional 122, 165
multi-pitch climbing 128, 134, 135
multi-pitch lowering 152-159
multi-pitch rappelling 142, 144-147
Munter hitch,
    described 32, 34
    for belaying off the anchor 126
Munter-mule159 (see also Munter hitch,
    mule knot)

N
natural anchors 96-105, 106-108, 132
    trees, evaluating 98, 99, using as rappel
        anchor 140, 141
    boulders, evaluating 98

nut 91, 92, 95, 122, 123, 131, 165
nut pick 95

O

objective hazards 63, 64
off fingers 115
off hands 116
ofwidth cracks 117, 118
on a bight 30, 31
open grip 39
opposition (protection placements) 123
oval carabiner 25, 26, 89, 90
overhand on a bight 31, 101, 156, 161
overhanging routes 80-83

P

pack 29
passive protection 91-92, 94
periodization 52
pinch grip 39
pitons 32, 90-91
pocket 40
protection (*see also* nut, SLCD) 90-95, 120,
    122-124, 135, 169
        cleaning 128, 131
        hex-shaped 91
        Tricams 92
        wedged-shaped 91, 92
prusik hitch 33, 34, 143, 144, 158, 159, 161,
    169-171
pulling the rope 83

Q

quick anchor 132
quick link 11
quickdraw 24, 26-28, 62, 71, 73, 84, 123

R

R rating 37
rack 89, 95, 96
rand 19

rappel ring 71, 73, 140, 141
rappelling 23, 32, 76-78, 133, 134, 139-150,
    156-158
        anchors 140, 141
        system backups 142-144
        ten commandments for safe 141, 142
        prerigged 145, 146, 149, 150, 153
        from a spider 146, 147, 150
reading the rock 55
redpointing 53
redundancy 99, 101, 105, 108
rescue 32, 122, 138, 139, 159
rest position 44,, 45, 55, 58
reversed and opposed carabiners 102, 103, 131
rock climbing, history of 12
rock shoes 19, 20
rope 17-19
rope core 17, 19
rope drag 120, 121
rope handling 46-49
rope sheath 17
RURP 16

S

sandbagging 66
seconding 128, 131
SECURE principles 96-99, 106-08
self-belay 34
shoes 19, 20
sidepull 40
single climbing ropes 17, 23
single rope 17
SLCD 92-94, 123, 124, 131, 165
slings 26, 71, 95, 123
        for improvised ascending 170
        on rappel anchor 141
slingshot belay 70-83, 127
slip-lasted 19, 20
slipper 20
smearing 44, 58, 118, 119
Spectra™ 27, 31

sport climbing 12, 26, 83-85
spotting 85
squeeze chimney 118
stacking the rope 84
standing end 30, 46
static elongation 18
static move (*compare to* dynamic move)
     41
static rope 17
stemming 41, 42, 58
stopper (*see* nut)
stopper knot 31
straight-gate carabiner 24, 26
strength training 53, 54, 58, 59
subjective hazards 64

T
tail 30
technique training 54-57
ten essentials 66, 67
test falls 18
third class 37
top-rope fall 18
top-roping 19,70-83
traditional climbing 28, 88, 89, 120-124
training with a partner 57
tramming 81

transitions 132-135
traverses & traversing 53, 80-83, 120, 123, 169
triple fisherman knot 27

U
UIAA 16, 18
undercling 40, 41
     used in lowering 152, 154, 155
     used during belay escapes 159, 161,
          163, 164

W
warming up 52, 53
water knot 27, 31, 32
webbing 27, 28, 74, 151
weight training 50-52
wire-gate carabiner 24

X
X rating 37

Y
Yosemite Decimal System 37
Yosemite National Park 12, 92

Z
zipper effect 120, 121

About the Authors

S. Peter Lewis has been a professional mountain guide since 1983. He is currently the marketing director and a rock and ice guide for the Eastern Mountain Sports Climbing School in North Conway, New Hampshire. He has also served as assistant director of the International Mountain Climbing School in North Conway and as executive director of the American Mountain Guides Association.

An award-winning photographer, Peter's work has appeared in several publications, including *Climbing* magazine, *Rock & Ice, Outside,* and *Backpacker.* Peter is also the author of *Toproping* (1998).

A native of Seattle, Washington, Dan Cauthorn first learned to climb in 1971 in the Washington Cascades. He began guiding and teaching climbing in 1979. In 1987, he was the co-founder of Vertical Club, the first indoor rock climbing gym in the nation. For ten years, Dan was the Director of Instruction at the gym, and during that time taught hundreds of people of all ages how to climb both indoors and outdoors. As a guide, Dan has led successful ascents of Denali, Aconcagua, Mount Waddington, and several big walls in Yosemite. An active climber on all types of terrain, Dan has also made major ascents on rock and ice throughout the world, from first ascents in Alaska to Patagonia's Cerro Torre. A frequent contributor to *Climbing* magazine, Cauthorn also wrote a chapter on training for climbing in The Mountaineers Books' title *Conditioning for Outdoor Fitness.* He lives in Seattle.